Addiction Is the Symptom

ADDICTION

IS THE

SYMPTOM

Heal the Cause and Prevent Relapse
with 12 Steps That Really Work

ROSEMARY ELLSWORTH BROWN, PhD
with LAURA MACKAY

Algorithm Books
www.algorithmbooks.com

ISBN-13: 978-0-9908208-0-2
LCCN: 2014916712

Distributed by Itasca Books

Book and cover design by Rebecca S. Neimark, Twenty-Six Letters

Printed in the United States of America

And if you're lost enough to find yourself
By now, pull in your ladder road behind you
And put a sign up CLOSED to all but me.
Then make yourself at home.

—From *Directive,* by Robert Frost

Contents

Preface

Addiction Is the Symptom is written from my perspective as a professional psychologist who, as a past member of Alcoholics Anonymous and other step groups, is intimately familiar with the twelve-step process. It is the result of research that I began in 1971 after a two-year relapse from AA. I had found my way to the program in 1968, but after a year, I was drinking again. When I returned to AA, I had just one objective: I did not want to experience another relapse.

Fast-forward to 1991. Intent on finding a solution to the problem of relapse, I had entered a doctoral program in which I was focused on the twelve-step process. Through the steps, I had been able to stop using alcohol, but I realized that I had relapsed in other ways, with other things—engaging, as so many people do, in what I came to call symptom substitution. Obviously, something was missing from the steps.

Through my research, I came to understand that relapse in one form or another was inevitable as long as treatment was directed at the addiction—the symptom—rather than its cause. So the question driving my research became not, "Why do people relapse?" but rather, "What causes addiction?" I reasoned that as with other diseases, if I could find the cause, a remedy might follow. As you shall see, I did find the cause, and a remedy did follow.

What pleases me most is that although my search started with the need to help myself, it turned out that the answers I found could help anyone with any kind of control issue—meaning almost everyone.

I have been asked many times how I managed to find these answers, and my reply is always the same: Not by myself.

First credit belongs to Alcoholics Anonymous. My critique of the program notwithstanding, there would be no book, perhaps even no life and work to record, if I had not been able to stop drinking through AA. Then too, the program was the beginning of my spiritual life, an ongoing and ever-evolving relationship with the God of my understanding. That this relationship has provided a creative and productive reflection in my life is unquestionable, and without it, again, there would be no book.

Next, I credit all the men and women struggling with addiction who helped me, through their failures and successes, to understand the importance of the fourth step. And further, all the clients and people I sponsored who were willing and able to complete with me what I now call the Fourth Step Algorithm, and who encouraged me to document how they achieved healing.

Many educators, researchers, and academic and professional mentors aided and encouraged my work over the years. I thank them all. A few of special note: Joan Garrett-Goodyear, one of my professors at Smith College, told me that my greatest gift was tenacity. "You are not satisfied with the surface of things," she said. "You have to dig further and find out why. It is a valuable quality." The compliment made me yet more tenacious. Dr. David S. Wyman, a brilliant scholar and a valued friend, was the first person to tell me I could write, and he encouraged me to do it. Dr. Paul Brenner suggested that I forget about publishing in a journal and instead put together a book for the general public. He told me that it was you, reading this right now, who needed to know what I knew. Dr. Jonas Salk, putting his arm around me at my going away party at the Salk Institute, told me, "I have found that if you can just live long enough, you can have it all." His remark reminded me to practice patience.

I must also thank my three children, who suffered with me during the agonizing years of addiction and ignorance, as I tried to understand what I needed to do to make life better for them and for me. They were not only my North Star, but also my motivation to keep going when I could find no other.

Finally, with regard to the book itself, I thank Kate Wilson and Mark Heitman for their careful and helpful reading of the manuscript, and Jonathan Caws-Elwitt for a precision copyedit. My former clients Carolena Wurmlinger and Mary MacKey repeatedly offered valuable feedback and support. Kim Bookless helped steer the book through the publishing process. Credit for the design goes to Rebecca Neimark. I also thank Scott Hancock for his excellent work filming my former clients' testimonials.

And of course there is Laura MacKay, my cowriter. I found Laura online on my eightieth birthday, when I woke up determined, once and for all, to get my work out into the larger world. Her writing, editing, and organizational skills, and her own considerable tenacity, made the results of my research accessible to you. Further, she inspired and sometimes nudged me to revisit and refine my ideas and my step method. The journey we have taken together has been more challenging and more rewarding than I could have imagined.

• • • • •

Facilitation Guidelines

*For professional therapists and counselors, companion facilitation guidelines are available for free download at **www.addiction-is-the-symptom.com**. The success of this twelve-step process depends on both how it is perceived and how it is executed. The facilitation guidelines concisely summarize the concepts that are the foundation of the Brown Method, detail the client screening process, and offer notes and advice on facilitating the Fourth Step Algorithm.*

Foreword

I had been sober continuously for over twenty-five years when Dr. Rosemary Brown first introduced me to her method for ending addiction in all its forms, with its focus on a precise working of AA's Step Four: "a searching and fearless moral inventory of ourselves."

I had taken a number of inventories over the years. They were good and cleansing, as they should be. Dr. Brown's method, however, was like a searchlight. It allowed me to reach into the very corners of my mind and my heart. With it, I took my first *truly* searching and fearless moral inventory.

As a result, I experienced freedom in my life as never before. Yes, I had been abstinent for many years, but I finally felt *healed*. Today, I have over forty-five years of continuous sobriety and a more joyful life full of happiness and humor. As an AA sponsor, I have also had the opportunity to guide people through Dr. Brown's method and subsequently to witness huge improvements in their lives as well.

Now Dr. Brown has outlined her method in this book.

Alcoholics Anonymous, known to many of us as the Big Book, was first published in April of 1939. Fourteen years later, in April 1953, Alcoholics Anonymous published *Twelve Steps and Twelve Traditions.* Since then, many individuals have written various self-help books for the millions who struggle with addiction—to alcohol, drugs, food, sex, relationships—so that they might work the Twelve Steps. But this is the only such book I know of that I believe is, like the Big Book and the *Twelve and Twelve,* divinely inspired. It is the chapter that's been missing from our recovery bible.

Dr. Brown's Fourth Step Algorithm, based on forty years of personal, professional, and academic research, is easy to understand and simple to follow. Fearlessly do the work. Watch your life unfold before you. You will at last get a clear picture of those hidden corners, of areas that you have flatly refused to look at over months or even, as in my case, years. You will reap the benefits in the form of the serenity and joy you long for.

—Len Baltzer, FACATA
Chemical dependency treatment consultant
Cofounder, National Association of Addiction Treatment Providers

Introduction

As one begins to understand oneself, that very beginning is the moment of freedom; and that is why it is very important not to have a guru, or make any book into an authority—because it is you who create authority, power, position. What is important is to understand yourself.

—J. Krishnamurti
Sixth Talk in Bombay, 1956

What is addiction? Over the course of a lifetime, I've experienced it personally, researched it academically, and, as a psychologist, treated it professionally. And I've come to define it more broadly than most: an addiction is any person, substance, or situation over which we have lost choice or believe we cannot live without—as evidenced by our continuing to consume or do or just want it despite the consequences for our health, mental state, family, and freedom.

Alcohol and other drugs, food, gambling, shopping, sex, relationships, money . . . We can develop an unhealthy emotional and often physical dependency on any one of these and more. You want to stop, but you can't. Or, sure, you can stop. Any time! But you can't stay stopped. The fact that you're reading this suggests that you know the feeling all too well. You've quit . . . many times. You start a new diet every Monday. You lost your paycheck at a poker game and cannot pay the rent. You went back to your abusive boyfriend again. Relapse, slip, backslide, fall off the wagon. Whatever you want to call it, it's demoralizing at best, life threatening at worst.

You are far from alone. Addiction is among the most pervasive and urgent problems of our time. Consider a few statistics for just substance addictions. In the United States in 2013, 8.2 percent of the population age twelve or older was classified with substance dependence or abuse.[1] One in six American adults admits to binge drinking,[2] and in 2010 alcohol caused nearly a third of all US vehicle fatalities.[3] While things like malaria and tuberculosis are still top concerns in the poorest countries, it is said that in most of the world, disease is now driven largely by overindulgence in alcohol, tobacco, and food.[4] Keeping in mind that not all obesity is caused by addiction (also at play are economic, environmental, and genetic factors, among others), obesity rates in 2008 were nearly double those of 1980; one in three adults were overweight (two out of three in the United States).[5]

These are dire numbers, yet I don't want to encourage you to think of addiction only in terms of extremes. It occurs on a spectrum, the whole of which is unhealthy. With regard to food, for example, we put anorexia at one end and obesity at the other, generally denying the area between. But anorexia and the typical weight-loss diet differ only in intensity. Anyone who goes on a diet has a problem with food—much the same way that anyone who goes on the wagon has a problem with alcohol. Many people are unaware that they have a problem until the object of their addiction is withdrawn, or threatened to be.

How do we end this? How do *you* end *your* addiction?

Traditionally, treatment has focused on one addiction at a time. Witness the proliferation of twelve-step groups not officially related to Alcoholics Anonymous since its founding in 1935. Codependents Anonymous, Gamblers Anonymous, Overeaters Anonymous, and Narcotics Anonymous are some of the best known, but there is an ever-expanding

---

[1] Substance Abuse and Mental Health Services Administration, "Results from the 2013 National Survey on Drug Use and Health: Summary of National Findings," NSDUH Series H-48, HHS Publication no. (SMA) 14-4863 (Rockville, MD): accessed 29 Oct. 2014, http://www.samhsa.gov/data/sites/default/files/NSDUHresultsPDFWHTML2013/Web/NSDUHresults2013.pdf.

[2] Jennifer Doren, "Sobering Stats on US Alcohol Consumption," *NBC Washington* (10 Jan. 2012): accessed 18 Jul. 2014, http://www.nbcwashington.com/news/health/Sobering-Stats-on-US-Alcohol-Consumption-137049283.html.

[3] The Century Council: accessed 18 Jul. 2014, http://www.centurycouncil.org/drunk-driving/drunk-driving-statistics.

[4] "Special Report: Obesity," *The Economist* (15 Dec. 2012): 78.

[5] Ibid., 15.

universe of others. The latest one I am aware of is Internet and Tech Addiction Anonymous (ITAA). Unfortunately, this glut of programs is not an indicator of success, as research has suggested for decades. Media reports and several recent books have finally begun to highlight this fact with regards to AA in particular. The numbers vary, but none are good. While the program is helpful to many people with alcohol addiction, at least seven out of ten participants relapse—they can't stay stopped.[6] Some research suggests that as many as *nine* out of ten will experience at least one relapse during the four years after treatment (which usually involves the steps); the rates are similar for nicotine and heroin addiction.[7] "Relapse is part of recovery," people often say. It's the norm.

The picture is even more discouraging when you account for the fact that many people who do manage to abstain from their substance, activity, or person of choice do so by substituting other addictions. At any substance recovery meeting (and in the course of forty years, I've probably been to upwards of two thousand), you will find plenty of coffee, cigarettes, and sugar. A twelve-step program can itself become a substitute addiction.

People call this recovery. In reality, it is only symptom management.

The limited success of twelve-step programs, and of addiction treatment in general, is due to an incomplete grasp of the problem. As I will share with you in detail in this book, single-addiction treatment doesn't work because *addiction is the symptom, not the problem*. The problem, common to all addiction, is an underlying *emotional dependency*. Its symptoms—addictive behaviors—are characterized by attempts to control and manipulate externals to meet internal emotional and spiritual needs. The fundamental dynamic is one of dependency on "the other," whatever or whomever that might be.

Where does emotional dependency come from? It's deeply conditioned during childhood. Now, don't think I'm blaming your mother; the parenting system is much bigger than any parent. It's a trap in which we are all caught. One that crosses time and culture. The objective of

---

[6] Norman K. Denzin, *The Alcoholic Society: Addiction and Recovery of the Self* (New Brunswick: Transaction Publishers, 1993), 275.

[7] National Institute on Alcohol Abuse and Alcoholism, no. 6 PH 277 (October 1989): accessed 18 Jul. 2014, http://pubs.niaaa.nih.gov/publications/aa06.htm.

this conditioning is control—the original addiction. And what better way to control children, to ensure their obedience, than to teach dependency? Dependency is readily achieved through rewards and punishments, and the fear they inspire. We never learn how to meet our own needs, only how to use others to get them met. Long before we ever take a drink or shoot up or start eating entire cartons of ice cream in one sitting, we become *users*. And to one degree or another, this is the model for *all* our relationships—with substances, with other people, even with ourselves. You don't have to have what most people would characterize as an addiction to find your life compromised by emotional dependency. It casts a long shadow.

I looked long and hard for the solution to all this. As it turned out, I needn't have looked far: it was hiding in the Twelve Steps all along. Through my many years of research, sponsoring people as a member of AA, and working as a psychologist in private practice, I developed a precise and truly comprehensive modification of the steps—let's call it the Brown Method—that addresses not only the symptoms but also the cause of addiction. It is essentially a spiritual process, but one with powerful psychological components. The result is a qualitative change in consciousness that is the foundation for *healing*. That is, you can leave relapse and mere symptom management behind. "Precise and comprehensive" is not what you will find in the myriad twelve-step programs. Rather, the general approach is to do the steps in your own time and in your own way. In other words, when you're "ready," and by trial and error. This approach is well suited to our addictive behaviors (think *control*: "No one can tell me what to do!"), but not to recovering from them.

As you'll see, I've modified the Twelve Steps in important ways that shift the primary focus from symptom to cause, starting with the foundational Step One. The heart of my method, the place where the real work gets done, is Step Four, "a searching and fearless moral inventory of ourselves." As I've modified it, it's an inventory of *all relationships,* and it concerns not so much how you may have hurt others, but rather the lifetime of hurts you yourself have suffered. It is the key to healing. Here, "precise and comprehensive" is particularly important. And so I devised the Fourth Step Algorithm: a set of specific instructions that empowers you to work the step with a facilitator—a professional therapist or counselor. Very little is left to chance. No more trial and error. And unlike conventional therapy, the algorithm is not about talking, but about working—for twenty to thirty minutes a day. Consequently, thanks to 21st-century technology, most of your interactions with your facilitator can happen at a distance, via phone, Skype, email, or text.

I won't tell you my step method is easy, but it is simple. Not to mention, in my considerable experience with sponsees (people who are sponsored, in program-speak) and clients, far more effective than the traditional steps.

Why does this process work? That question is best answered by doing it, but the short answer is this: because it is the beginning of self-parenting, and therefore of healthy self-reliance, also known as freedom. Through these modified steps, particularly the fourth and fifth, you become acutely aware of the unconscious conditioning that's been driving your addictive behaviors. Your learned dependency becomes the independence that is your birthright as you learn instead to turn to a higher power within for what you need. Most of all, you begin a lifelong journey of spiritual self-discovery that is the foundation of healing.

What I'm telling you is that you can heal yourself of addiction. I should say that if you're addicted to chemicals, this doesn't mean it will magically become safe for you to use; it means you'll be able to stay stopped and feel good doing it. Whatever your addiction, or to whatever extent emotional dependency is running your life, you will regain choice. You will no longer have an addiction, in the broadest, deepest sense of the word. I myself am testament to this, along with my clients, seven of whom (Chris, Alex, Carolena, Jen, Ernie, Joan, and Paul) you'll meet in these pages.

Yes, I know . . . this directly contradicts everything many of us have been told about addiction, to alcohol in particular ("You don't graduate from the program"). Consequently, my work has not always been well received by people who are addicted or my peers in the treatment business. It's been a struggle to get this book published. But just because a disease is labeled "chronic" or "incurable" does not mean that it can't be healed, only that no one has yet figured out how to do it. It's taken me a lifetime, but I have figured out how to do it. This book is meant to empower you to do it too. I invite you to begin your own journey of self-understanding and self-healing.

If you find that you are not ready to take that journey, I hope you will take one thing from this book: you are not your addictive behavior. There is nothing wrong with *you*. What's wrong is all the garbage—the conditioning—piled on top of you. Take that thought to the mirror each morning, and try, for even a moment, to see who you really are. Not "an addict," "an alcoholic," "a binge eater," "a sexaholic," or whatever false identity you've been saddled with. No. A person. And a beautiful one at that.

Summary

· An addiction is any person, process, substance, or situation over which we have lost choice or believe we cannot live without.

· People who have addictions have lost choice. Specifically, they want to permanently stop doing something destructive, but can't.

· Traditional single-addiction treatment inevitably results in some form of relapse because addiction is the symptom, not the problem.

· The underlying problem, the problem common to all addictions, is emotional dependency.

· Emotional dependency is conditioned by our parenting system, whose objective is control (the original addiction), and thus plagues almost everyone to some degree.

· Emotional dependency is the model for *all* our relationships—with substances, with other people, even with ourselves.

· Emotional dependency can be unlearned through the modification of the Twelve Steps outlined in this book—the Brown Method—which systematically brings your unconscious conditioning to consciousness, thus restoring choice.

Part 1

The Foundation

Chapter 1

My Name Is . . .

For, while the tale of how we suffer, and how we are delighted, and how we may triumph is never new, it always must be heard. There isn't any other tale to tell, it's the only light we've got in all this darkness.

—James Baldwin
Sonny's Blues

My name is Rosemary. I used to be addicted. As of April 15, 2014, I've been sober for forty-three years. My tale of addiction is less important than that of my healing—which came long after my sobriety—but I'll share it nonetheless.

Fifteen

I got drunk for the first time in 1947, at age fifteen. It was after a dance. It was winter. I was wearing a beautiful dress, and I sat down in a snowdrift. I can still see myself laughing uproariously. Everyone else was laughing, at what I don't know . . . perhaps at nothing. It's a lovely, silly memory. It was mere adolescent overindulgence, really.

The second time I got drunk was a different story. It was the night of my high school graduation. Graduation wasn't much fun. I don't know what I expected, but whatever it was, it didn't happen. What did happen was I fell down a flight of stairs in the home of a friend. When she told me the next day, I felt so remorseful. I made a general apology to cover that and anything else I might have done: I didn't remember the fall, or much of the evening for that matter. It was only the first time I would apologize for something I could not remember.

For all kinds of reasons, life in the little Pennsylvania steel town I grew up in was hard from day one. I think I'll save all that for my auto-biography. Suffice it to say, it's no surprise that I would have an inclination to drive away pain with alcohol. Or an inclination to marry much too young, in hopes of escape. But of course I could not escape myself.

An Era of Pill Popping

Despite my early blackout experience, my first real addiction was to pills, although I did not recognize it at the time. After the birth of my second child, in March 1957, I suffered a severe depression. I couldn't shake it. It's possible that I had what we now recognize as postpartum depression. I was twenty-five years old, and all I knew was that something inside me was terribly broken. I felt shattered. I could talk to no one. So about three months after my daughter was born, I turned for help to the doctor who had delivered her.

This was the beginning of an era of pill popping, culturally speaking. Tranquilizers hadn't been on the market for very long. "New ones coming out every day," the doctor told me. I remembered laughing with someone at work when he said that before he went in to see his boss, he popped a Milltown—the original "mother's little helper." It was very fashionable. And now here was my doctor saying, "Well, you can go away for a while" (which I translated to mean, "you can *put yourself away* for a while"), "or you can try some tranquilizers that may help your depression." Since I had no place to go, and with two children to care for couldn't very well go if I did, I opted for the pills.

None of us knew then that we were guinea pigs, that our doctors were prescribing medications without knowing their full effects. My doctor prescribed the wrong drug, Stelazine—a high-potency antipsychotic used to alleviate anxiety, agitation, and psychosis—at the highest dosage. He also prescribed diet pills to help me lose weight. I took the latter only briefly because while I was on them, I couldn't sleep for any length of time. But I continued to take my little blue Stelazines every day, one in the morning and one at night. "They will make you feel better," the doctor had told me. And they did make me feel better. They made me not feel at all. But what mattered was that I could still function. I could still work. And life went on.

Just a month or so later, my husband got a teaching job at an exclusive private boarding school. It was a wonderful opportunity. The headmaster was also looking for a school secretary, and he was delighted that, as he put it, he could get "two for one." So the four of us moved into an ivy-covered house just across the lawn from the main building of the lovely campus.

The experience would undoubtedly have been very different if not for the tranquilizers I was taking—and if I hadn't started drinking. In this new world, social drinking on the weekends was the norm in our circle. In a short time, drinking became habitual, along with the pills. For the first time, I began keeping alcohol in the house. It was years before people would be advised not to drink alcohol in combination with certain medications. The general public first learned about the dangers via reports of celebrities dying from compound effects. I had no awareness of myself or the process in which I was engaged. The downward spiral that ensued was guaranteed, between the pills and the alcohol and the history I brought with me.

Where I came from, socioeconomic boundaries were carved in stone. Now here I was, a working-class girl suddenly on the right side of the tracks. I was in awe of the social environment in which I found myself. Founded over one hundred years before, the school was a place of tradition where family trees meant a great deal. My family background, or rather lack of one—I was adopted—loomed large. I was determined to learn my new part as fast as I could, and within a few months, six at the outside, I looked, spoke, and acted as though I belonged.

Outwardly, I had become one of the privileged class. Inwardly, though, I was in terror that someone would find out that I was not what I seemed. A friend later recast my deception as a talent, pointing out that I had learned in a few months what everyone around me had acquired from childhood. If only I had experienced it that way at the time. As it was, for the next four years, I believed that I was living a lie. Others found me reserved, even haughty. I said very little. I observed. I had no real friends. I did what I was required to do, and I did it extremely well. In retrospect, it is clear that from this point on, I became whatever the environment required. I had no self. It would be close to a lifetime before I felt satisfied with who I was or what I had.

By the end of our second year at the school, I was drinking heavily every weekend and had my share of blackouts and hangovers. I started covering up the smell on my breath with mints or, occasionally, a spoonful of peanut butter. Meanwhile, thanks to the Stelazine, I had difficulty distinguishing reality from fantasy. Yet I maintained peak efficiency.

By the time we moved from the East Coast to the West Coast in 1961, for my husband's career in academia, I had read about the dangers of combining pills and alcohol. Within the first month of our move, I stopped taking the pills, but I immediately started drinking even more to compensate for the withdrawal. I was totally unaware of the switch I was making. Within a month or two I was drinking daily. California was Mecca for me. All those wine tastings! Not to mention all the entertaining among faculty members. Drinks before dinner, wine with dinner, after-dinner wine or liqueur, and then a nightcap or two after you went home. The hiding started—having friends over for sherry and lacing mine with vodka. Camping and alcohol went together very nicely too, or so I thought at the time.

I had lost choice. I recognized that there was a problem, but I couldn't do anything about it. I was able to stop drinking during my third pregnancy only because the addiction had not progressed to the point where my need to drink overrode my desire to have a healthy child. After my son was born, I began drinking again, and it soon escalated. As high as my consumption was during this period, I was able to control myself enough to hide it from the outside world. I could still function. I could still work. It was 1963.

Learning Not to Drink

I went to my first Alcoholics Anonymous meeting in 1968, shortly after my thirty-fifth birthday. I had quit drinking a couple of months before, and one afternoon it occurred to me that not drinking was a very lonely business. There weren't any treatment centers then. Well, maybe a few, but none that I had heard about. If you had the money and a doctor's referral, you could go to a private hospital to dry out under a fake diagnosis. I had neither, so I looked in the Yellow Pages, where I found a number for the central Alcoholics Anonymous office.

I knew nothing about AA. I had never thought about it before. But I immediately felt at home. As I met people in the Fellowship to whom I could relate, my loneliness abated. No matter our backgrounds, we understood each other in a way that transcended our differences. It has been said, and I have often found it to be true, that the language of the heart is spoken in AA, that words really don't matter. The communication is heart to heart instead of mind to mind. Time and again at meetings, I heard, "Our best thinking brought us through the doors of AA. Until we learn how to think with our hearts, we have little chance for a healthier life." It was in AA that I learned how not to drink, but more importantly, it was the place where I learned the practical meaning of love: to give with no expectations.

For months I attended meetings regularly. I didn't work the steps, but I wasn't drinking either. I did gain weight, however. Sugar is a natural substitute for alcohol. Then I started an exercise program, which was quite an accomplishment, since I am not at all athletically inclined. It took about a month for it to become just another addiction, although I certainly did not see it as such at the time. My daily routine included an early morning TV exercise program followed by a two-mile jog at the beach. (By now we had moved to the beachside community of La Jolla.) At lunch, I occasionally swam laps. Two nights a week, I went to an additional exercise class. I felt terrible if I missed a day of my routine, and if I did I tried to make it up. After about nine months of this, I became bored with the whole thing and stopped.

At no time during this period did I pay much attention to working the Twelve Steps beyond Step One, nor did anyone encourage me to. Not directly, anyway. This mistake is all too common in twelve-step programs, where a "when you're ready" attitude prevails. Still, I became healthier, if only physically. And the healthier and more clear-headed I became, the more I realized how sick my marriage was. I demanded and got a divorce.

I'd been in AA for about a year when, at a meeting that I was leading, I thanked everyone and told them that this meeting was my last, that I had decided I didn't need the program any longer. I was confident that I would not be visiting those rooms again. I looked great. I felt great. I thought I had it together. For about two weeks I enjoyed the frequent calls from my AA friends and being able to tell them, "I'm happy to report that I was right. I don't have a problem."

Then I fell apart. At first, it was one drink when I got home from work. "See," I told myself, "you can handle it. No problem." Then the headaches came, because after the first drink I wanted another one but resisted. I knew that if I had another one, I had a problem, so for a week or two I put up with the headaches. I pretended not to notice that the "one drink" was now going into the largest glass I had. From the moment I picked up the first drink, I didn't want to talk to or hear from anyone in AA. When they called, I told them that I was too busy to talk.

On April 15, 1971, I woke up sometime in the early morning hours. I was stretched out on the couch, uncovered and cold. My neck hurt. My head hurt. I felt dirty. I smelled. It took a very long time for me to open my eyes. The living room was in darkness except for the light of the television, and it seemed very far away. At that hour, there was no program on, just snow. I noticed a reflection in the screen: the outline of the skillet on the coffee table. Had I eaten? Had I used a fork? I didn't see a fork. Had the kids watched me eat with my fingers? No. I always waited until they were asleep before I did any serious drinking. There was an empty half-gallon wine jug on the floor. "I'll have to get that out of here," I thought. Even though I was barely conscious, I knew I didn't want the kids to see it. I somehow made my way to the kitchen, first with the skillet, then with the jug, which I shoved down under the garbage. I slowly and carefully crawled up the stairs and managed to get into bed.

After waking up, stumbling through a quick shower, and getting ready for work, I found myself in front of the phone on the wall. "What are you doing standing here in front of the phone?" I asked myself. "Who do you want to call at this hour?" The answer was Will Campbell, an AA friend. I hadn't talked to him in the two years since I'd left AA. He wouldn't care what time it was.

That morning was no different from any other . . . There was absolutely no reason why I would make that call. I can only describe it as a moment of grace. I haven't had a drink since.

A Parade of Addictions

In the spring of my first year back in AA, I had somehow saved enough money to take the children out for fish and chips. It's hard to describe what that meant to me. Anyone reading this who has experienced chemical addiction knows what I'm talking about. It was something

Addiction Is the Symptom

that I had been wanting to do for a couple of years, but I'd never been able to get myself together to do it. It was so special for me—to know that I wouldn't be drinking, that I wouldn't embarrass them or myself. It was raining that night, and I remember getting out of the car and starting to cry. I smelled the earth. It smelled fresh, green. I felt so grateful just to be alive and to be there with my three beautiful, hungry children. A simple moment, but one I'll never forget.

Yet along with my abstinence came a growing awareness that something remained terribly wrong. I could not fathom why I continued to feel, much of the time, like an active alcoholic. I was doing my best to follow the program. I eventually worked through the steps a number of times, in accordance with the interpretations of my sponsors. What was I doing wrong? What was wrong with *me*? I could not help but notice that many AA "old-timers" relapsed or committed suicide. These were people who served as examples to newcomers of what worked, people who appeared to be doing everything right, some with long-term sobriety. I myself held on to abstinence not because I wanted to live, but because I had three children who depended on me for their survival.

I did not know then that I was still in the throes of addiction. That I could abstain from alcohol only because I had substituted other addictions for it—beginning with AA itself. The result was a long and painful parade of substitute addictions. After my return to AA, it took about a month for me to begin a relationship with a man, someone else in the program. Then there was exercise, cigarettes, work. My children bore the brunt of this. I was no more present to them without alcohol than I had been before. All that had changed was the mode of expression. I found myself going from one twelve-step group to another in an attempt to deal with each addiction as it surfaced. My self-loathing and the pain that my addictions caused my children brought me to the brink of despair.

I would come to learn that as addiction progresses, we attempt to control ourselves with an unbelievable intensity so that no one (including ourselves) will recognize how bad off we really are. In the early stage of recovery, it is no different. We are conscious once more, and added to the fear are shame and contempt. Unless these are addressed through the Twelve Steps, they only grow, and the emotional pain becomes so great that we must relapse, slowly killing ourselves with the same or another addiction. Or quickly, as many do.

Years went by, and despite everything, I was grateful for my abstinence. It seemed like a miracle. In the first months, it had been difficult to even hold a single thought. I was alone in supporting myself and my children, so I was desperate to keep my job. I would compel myself to stare at a pencil or any other object on my desk in order to focus, to collect my thoughts, so I could concentrate on the task at hand. I remember too sitting at home with a simple mystery novel, reading the same paragraph over and over again, unable to comprehend it. Reading had always been my great love. I broke out in a cold sweat and threw the book at the wall in frustration.

• • • • •

Yet thirteen years later, in 1984, I was accepted into the Ada Comstock program for nontraditional students at Smith College. At age fifty-one, I was going to college for the first time.

In 1989, I graduated from Smith with a BA in English. But at around the same time, my addictions came to a head. I found myself checking into a treatment center for twenty-eight days—but not for alcohol addiction. No, I was there for an equally deadly form of dependency: a relationship addiction, what was newly recognized as codependency.

Years later when I spoke at seminars on the subject of codependency, the audience would laugh when I closed with the admonition, "Remember, when two hearts beat as one, someone is dead—don't let it be you." But it was no laughing matter at the time. During my stay at the treatment center, I experienced emotional and physical symptoms painfully similar to those I had experienced while withdrawing from alcohol. It wasn't the first time I had been through withdrawal, but it was particularly intense, perhaps because of my sheer dismay: How was it that I found myself in a treatment program for codependency after working so hard on the program for the last eighteen years? After sponsoring scores of people? I began to glimpse the idea that my addictive behavior was caused by my emotional dependency. Until I could find a way to heal that core problem of how I related to myself, others, and the world in general, I would never be free of addictions.

And that, my dear friend, was the beginning of the end of my tale of suffering. The rest of this book concerns my triumph—my healing—and quite possibly yours.

Chapter 2

Addiction Is the Symptom, Not the Problem

I finally get it. Even though I'm not using alcohol or other drugs, I'm still using. I'm using sex, I'm using other people, the same way I used drugs, to get my needs met.
—Narcotics Anonymous member

When I was new to Alcoholics Anonymous, I, like other members of AA and members of twelve-step programs in general, assumed that if I did everything I was supposed to do, the "Promises" in the Big Book* (page 83) would come true:

> If we are painstaking about this phase of our development, we will be amazed before we are half way through. We are going to know a new freedom and a new happiness. We will not regret the past nor wish to shut the door on it. We will comprehend the word *serenity* and we will know peace. No matter how far down we have gone, we will see how our experience can benefit others. That feeling of uselessness and self-pity will disappear. We will lose interest in selfish things and gain interest in our fellows. Self-seeking will slip away. Our whole attitude and outlook upon life will change. Fear of people and of economic insecurity will leave us. We will intuitively know how to handle situations which used to baffle us. We will suddenly realize that God is doing for us what we could not do for ourselves.

---

* *Alcoholics Anonymous,* aka the Big Book (fourth edition), and *Twelve Steps and Twelve Traditions,* aka the *Twelve and Twelve,* are published by Alcoholics Anonymous World Services Inc. (New York, 2002). AAWS asked that the following statement be included in this book, to which I agreed: "The A.A. material reprinted in this publication is a fair use, that is the A.A. material reprinted is not substantial."

I wanted all of that, and I was willing to work for it. After my ninety meetings in ninety days, I kept going to meetings, talked at those meetings, got a sponsor, read the literature, sponsored others, did service, worked the steps in the way that I thought worked for me, gained an understanding of a power greater than myself, practiced rigorous honesty, and of course did not drink. Eventually, I even served for a year as a consultant to an educational program focusing on early identification of addictive behavior, giving seminars and workshops in schools and for community organizations.

Yet, like the majority of twelve-step participants (including my clients Chris and Alex, introduced in the pages that follow), I discovered that the Promises were elusive. I was far from "amazed." I was amazingly unhappy. I did not know serenity or peace. For too many people, even abstinence is elusive; as noted earlier, at least seven out of ten AA participants start drinking again.

AA meetings often begin with this announcement: "Let us have a moment of silence for the alcoholic who still suffers." During these early years, whenever I joined in that moment, the object of my thoughtful silence was the person outside the program. The one who never had the choice of recovery and was still doomed to the life of an "addict." One night I realized that "the alcoholic who still suffers" was not only the one who had never made it to the program, but also the one who *had* and, for one reason or another, remained miserable after months or years. The alcoholic who still suffered was me.

A Learning Curve

My first inkling of what was going on occurred several years after my relapse into drinking and return to AA. As I described in chapter 1, I'd begun going from step group to step group in an attempt to deal with the series of new addictions that surfaced after I became sober. I also simply wanted to learn as much as I could. Due to the popularity of Alcoholics Anonymous, twelve-step groups were rapidly multiplying at the time, so I had plenty to choose from. I had AA friends who also went to Narcotics Anonymous, and I started going with them. At one NA meeting, a man stood and said this:

I finally get it. Even though I'm not using alcohol or other drugs, I'm still using. I'm using sex, I'm using other people, the same way I used drugs, to get my needs met—a physical fix instead of a chemical one to ease the loneliness, to dull the pain, to make me forget even for a few moments how much I hate myself. The pressure builds, and I know one of these days I'll have to relieve it one way or another, a slow suicide through drugs or a fast one by some other means.

I had never before thought about "using" in this way. But even though I was doing it myself, the fact didn't quite click for me, because it didn't fit my mental framework. Even today, twelve-step programs are organized around a single addiction, and talking about other addictions is discouraged or outright disallowed. It's all about whatever addiction brought you in. It would be years before I realized what an astute observation that man had made. However, through NA I did realize that my first addiction had been to pills.

Chris   AA was my first twelve-step membership. I stayed sober and went to meetings, and when I'd become full of resentments and fears, I'd write them out and share them because that practice seemed to help. However, although I was not drinking or drugging, I was acting out with other addictions.

When I hit bottom with codependency, I never thought I'd live long enough to write about it. It wasn't a gradual process. It occurred during a phone call with my lover (read Higher Power). He admitted he was having an affair and wasn't certain about the future of our relationship. I went from being a highly functional, highly educated, long-sober member of AA to a terrified, non-functioning mass of teardrops. I didn't think I'd have to commit suicide, because I thought my pain would kill me. I was at that point without a job, without a home, without an ounce of hope.

Hadn't I done everything correctly up to then? I had gone to AA meetings, done service, worked the steps, not drank or drugged for thirteen years. I saw AA as the be-all, end-all of life. I didn't realize that more growth was necessary. I continued to "live" hanging on by a thread.

> Alex   I had been sober for more than eight years, going to AA
>   meetings and sponsoring as well as having a sponsor. In
> addition, I had attended Overeaters Anonymous, Debtors Anony-
> mous, Al-Anon, and then lastly Codependents Anonymous.
>
> Still at the core of me I felt like a victim of life and of life's cir-
> cumstances, and inferior to most other people. All the twelve-step
> programs I experienced never healed me from my using; it was
> only sublimated. The drink or drug, I abstained from, but in its
> place came overworking, sex, shopping, relationships, and the list
> goes on.

I finally started to "get it" more than a dozen years later, after my treatment for codependency. I left the treatment center determined to find a solution to the problem of dependency—meaning dependency on any*one* or any*thing*. In the early 1990s, I entered a graduate program in counseling psychology and focused my academic research on discovering why Alcoholics Anonymous and its growing number of clones proved ineffective for the majority of their members—that is, why relapse was the norm. There was something right with the twelve-step process. Of that I was certain. But something was wrong too. What, exactly? And how might it be remedied?

My doctoral committee included Dr. Paul Wood, who was chairman of the National Council on Alcoholism and Drug Dependence (NCADD), and Jerry Spicer, who at the time was the controller at Hazelden, the famed nonprofit treatment organization founded on AA principles. He went on to serve as president. In addition, I chose three facilitators in the field, one whose specialty was art as therapy and another who had done considerable research on religion as addiction. I was also privileged to have support and substantial input from Dr. Elisabeth Kübler-Ross, the renowned pioneer of near-death studies.

With my academic research, I cast a broad net. It encompassed on-site visits to treatment centers and hospitals; interviews with directors, employees, and patients within those treatment facilities; a comparison survey of the ways in which the Twelve Steps were offered to patients in over one hundred treatment centers; and an analysis of various treatment center outcome evaluations. Given my growing suspicion that all addictions were connected, my efforts were not limited to alcohol addiction. I completed a comparison study of three well-known diet programs and, less formally, continued to attend a variety of twelve-step meetings. Narcotics Anonymous, Overeaters Anonymous, Emotions Anonymous, Gamblers Anonymous, and others. And through AA, I had countless sponsorship encounters.

Over time, I noticed the same thing again and again: symptom substitution.

Symptom Substitution

The word *relapse* was commonly used, and continues to be used by many, when someone who is addicted to alcohol returns to drinking. But few had recognized the substitution of a different addiction as a form of relapse. Further, few recognized—as the wise man at that NA meeting did—that nonchemical dependencies were addictions. But this is very important to understand: addiction is addiction. The less obvious dependencies can be easier to deny or ignore. A person with an eating disorder can appear healthy and in good shape. Some addictions (workaholism, for one) are even encouraged. An addiction is usually not recognized as such until the object of the dependency is removed and the emotional and/or physical symptoms of withdrawal are set in motion.

My study of the diet programs clearly demonstrated the correspondence between substance addictions and what we psychologists now call process addictions: addictions not to a chemical but to a process or activity, such as working, eating (although research indicates that certain foods, notably sugar, have druglike qualities), gambling, shopping, or sex. Today, brain research is affirming these similarities, showing that substance and process addictions have comparable effects on neurotransmitters. With the diet programs, one similarity was that dieters could take weight off but often could not keep it off, which I concluded made many of them no different from people who could stop drinking but could not stay stopped—they relapsed.*

---

*A caveat here. Let's bear in mind that any number of people in weight loss programs may be there not because they actually need to lose weight, but because they are in the grips of a false standard that says they should.

Armed with all this research (and a PhD), I began to see the clients who came through the door of my private counseling practice more clearly.

One day, a 6 a.m. phone call from a man seeking help for his wife led to an aha moment. He wanted to bring her over for a consultation immediately because of the difficult night he had just experienced due to her drinking. I said yes and made some coffee. When they arrived, we sat down to discuss the wife's problem with alcohol. It was obvious that when this man talked about his wife's addiction, his larger concern was his inability to concentrate on his work, which, he said, "commands all my time." I soon realized that before me sat two addicted people: one addicted to alcohol and one to work. One addiction was known to be a blight on society; the other was considered a virtue. I also saw that regardless of the addiction, the families share a similar fate. In each instance, the addicted person is not available. In each instance, children get the message that something is more important than they are, which engenders the same feelings of rejection and low self-worth. Addiction is addiction.

Consider one longstanding definition of alcoholism, that of the National Council on Alcoholism and Drug Dependence and the American Society of Addiction Medicine:

> It is characterized by impaired control over drinking, preoccupation with the drug alcohol, use of alcohol despite adverse consequences, and distortions in thinking, most notably denial. Each of these symptoms may be continuous or periodic.[8]

Now insert whatever substance or behavior you've lost choice over:

> It is characterized by impaired control over [work, food, sex, shopping, gambling . . .], preoccupation with _____, use of _____ despite adverse consequences, and distortions in thinking, most notably denial.

The definition works regardless of the form your addiction takes, does it not?

The way in which alcoholism is segregated from other addictions in our language, both formally and informally, encourages confusion in

---

[8] *Journal of the American Medical Association,* 1992:268, 1012–1014.

this matter. Alcohol is, in fact, a drug. Yet the standard phraseology is "alcohol and drugs." There's the National Council on Alcoholism and Drug Dependence. There's the National Clearing House for Alcohol and Drug Information. Police forms refer to "alcohol and/or drugs." AA members can be heard to say, "Oh no, I didn't take drugs. I just drank." The correct phrasing is "alcohol and *other* drugs" or "drugs, *including* alcohol." It's a convenient oversight, one that reflects alcohol's legality and social acceptability. It fosters the specific illusion that addiction to alcohol is somehow not as serious as addiction to other drugs, and the general illusion that the various addictions are fundamentally different.

With all that in mind, let's now consider the other piece of that "official" definition of alcoholism:

> A primary, chronic disease with genetic, psychosocial, and environmental factors influencing its development and manifestations. The disease is often progressive and fatal.

"Often progressive and fatal." Unfortunately, this part of the definition also applies regardless of the form your addiction takes. (As you know, I believe I have disproved "chronic.") Any substance or behavior that takes over your life can compromise it to the point of death, if indirectly. Heroin might kill you faster than, say, sugar, but sugar can eventually do the job via diabetes and other complications of obesity.

• • • • •

Once I recognized the fundamental equality of addictions—as I hope you now do—the phenomenon of symptom substitution became visible. Sugar for alcohol, overeating for cigarettes, dieting and exercise for overeating, and serial relationships for sex are just some of the most common substitutions/relapses; the configurations are endless. Evidently, addictions are more or less interchangeable. People who are "in recovery" are too often only *re-covering,* or covering up, a primary addiction with one or more substitutes.

Is it any wonder that single-addiction treatment, such as that offered by twelve-step groups, does not work very well? Imagine if only the symptoms of cancer were treated—aspirin for the pain, Valium for psychic anguish, etc.—while the cancer, the cause of it all, continued to grow and metastasize.

Even a twelve-step program can serve as a substitute for the more obvious addiction it's meant to address. The sponsor-sponsee relationship that is integral to twelve-step programs, however well intentioned, plays a significant role in this symptom substitution. It encourages a new but essentially similar dependency, this time on another person's advice about how to do the program, how to work the steps, and how to live your life. (You may well ask, "Isn't this text *Dr. Brown's* personal advice on doing the steps?" The answer is yes. However, as you will see, there are major differences in this approach that prevent such dependency. And then there is the different outcome: healing instead of relapse.)

Many will object to this or say that if a twelve-step program is an addiction, it's a far healthier one. However, recognizing all symptom substitution for what it is—relapse—is important in part because, again, addiction is progressive and often fatal. Denial only aids its progression. It's also my experience that people who relapse into nonchemical addictions are prone to returning to chemical abuse of some sort.

Every time you relapse, discrimination lessens, and with time, disappears. If your addiction is to alcohol, you begin with a taste for a particular drink, a special brand. Eventually, when asked, "What'll you have?" the answer is, "Whatever you've got." If your addiction is to relationships, you start out with a certain kind of person in mind—good-looking, up-and-coming, motivated, kind, funny. Eventually—and this is particularly noticeable if the addiction is to sex—any body will do. If your addiction is to food, the special dessert you once reached for, the comfort food you preferred, becomes anything you can quickly stuff in your mouth. In every case, the ultimate result may be early death. You drive into a tree, you contract HIV, you end up with diabetes . . . The older we grow, the harsher the reality.

Emotional Dependency

If addictions are so readily interchangeable, then they must have something in common, right? And that something must be the real problem, not the act of drinking or overeating or what have you, although those behaviors must of course stop.

Through my research and my personal experience, I finally came to see that what all addictions have in common is *emotional dependency.* This may sound obvious. After all, the word *dependency* is used all the time in relation to addiction. But when at some point I recognized my codependency as *emotional* dependency, I suddenly recognized *that* dependency as the problem behind the problem—and as the common cause of all addictions. All our relationships are emotion-based, not just those we have with people. It was a hard connection to make only because twelve-step programs, and indeed the entire treatment industry, were focused—blindly so—on individual symptoms. For the most part, they still are. *Emotional dependency* accurately describes the nature of addiction itself. And it is this core dependency that is acted out with whatever or whoever is available to you.

The next question on my journey to recovery, then, was this: Where does emotional dependency come from? The entire premise of addiction treatment was and is that addictions cannot be healed, only treated. But if all addictions were just symptoms of the single problem of emotional dependency . . . then perhaps the key to healing could be found in the *cause* of this problem.

Key Concepts

Symptom substitution The substitution of one form of addictive behavior for another (sugar for alcohol, dieting for overeating . . .).

Relapse Traditionally defined as a return to using your substance of choice. In truth, however, the substitution of a second, third, or fourth choice of substance, person, or process in order to maintain abstinence from the first is a form of relapse.

Emotional dependency Reliance on that which is outside ourselves for our emotional needs. It's the underlying problem that all addictions have in common.

Abstinence Not synonymous with healing. It addresses only the symptom and often coexists with symptom substitution. If you have not recovered from your underlying emotional dependency, you are vulnerable to substituting an equally or more life-threatening addiction for your drug of choice.

Chapter 3

The Roots of Addiction

The way out of a trap is to know the way the trap is built. Only then will it cease being a trap.
—Willard and Marguerite Beecher
Beyond Success and Failure

I was a fat little girl. My parents forced me to eat everything they put on my plate. Everything, every time, without fail. I was not allowed to choose how much I ate, let alone what I ate. Choices were not for children. If I ate what I was told to eat, I received a reward; if I didn't, I was punished. I grew so fat that I couldn't fit into regular children's clothes and had to go to a store in a larger town that had a department for "chubbies." On the other hand, when on occasion I hadn't had enough to eat, I would ask for more and usually be told, "You can't be hungry, you just ate." In time, I stopped asking.

It's an extreme example of the timeworn dinner-table battle, some form of which many of us grew up with. The battle needn't be extreme to have its effect, though. Think about it: the message to a child is that she can't trust her own sense of hunger or taste.

The dynamic is about control. And not only the superficial control of determining what a child eats. The best way to control someone is to make him or her dependent on you. The child who learns that she can't trust her own hunger (or other feelings and judgments beyond the dinner table) may come to believe, as I did, that she can't trust any of her feelings and desires. That she must depend on her parents, and later, others, not only for her basic needs, but also for her very sense of self.

Unfortunately, parenting as we know it rests on this dynamic, whether it is subtle or extreme. That is, parenting is typically more about control—about creating dependence—than about love.

A Vicious Circle

As I searched for the cause of emotional dependency, it was only natural to turn to childhood, and in turn to parenting. My own childhood, as you may have gathered by now, was an inspiration of sorts. But also, by the time I embarked on my graduate research, I was thoroughly steeped in the work of the groundbreaking psychologist Alice Miller.

With such books as *For Your Own Good* (1980) and *Thou Shalt Not Be Aware* (1981), Miller became a harsh critic of parenting's abuses, including the corporal punishment that too many parents view as their right. Miller saw the roots of worldwide adult violence in the fact that children are beaten, especially during their early years when the brain is still forming. They can't defend themselves against the violence done to them, so they suppress their rage and fear—only to discharge them against their peers or, once they become adults, against their own children and even whole peoples (think Hitler, whose childhood Miller famously analyzed). Simply put, they become bullies. It's a vicious circle. As Miller said, "The reason why parents mistreat their children has less to do with character and temperament than with the fact that they too were mistreated and were not permitted to defend themselves."[9]

Miller's work, along with that of people like Anne Wilson Schaef, Diane Fassel, Ira Hyman, and Philip Greven, spoke to the extraordinary power of the parent-child relationship to shape each of us and, further, the world. Consequently, many of us in the field of psychology were seeing this power more clearly than ever before. I came to understand that the vicious circle of violence was not the only one fueled by the parenting system: emotional dependency, too, was learned and passed from generation to generation, and reinforced by our educational, religious, cultural, and political institutions.

It should be obvious enough that to a child, parents can be gods or monsters (usually something in between). Your parents can give gifts, or they can take them away. They can help you or hurt you. If you do as you're told, you are rewarded. Rebel, and you are punished. You know at a tender age that your very life depends on them. Perhaps less obvious is how you, as a child, responded to all this. With fear and intelli-

---

[9] Alice Miller, *For Your Own Good* (New York: Noonday Press, 1990), 105.

Addiction Is the Symptom

gence, it turns out: you became expert at figuring out what your parents needed or wanted in the hope that once they were satisfied, they in turn would meet your needs.

Too often, what parents want, if unconsciously, is to dominate and control—they themselves having survived the same fear-based, power-oriented parenting model. Obedience is achieved through the manipulation of rewards and punishments. It's an animal training model for human beings, one that becomes the model for all your relationships. The extent to which you experience this conditioning, which begins in infancy, is the extent to which you become emotionally dependent—and consequently engage in addictive behavior.

It should be understood that I'm not advocating a lack of structure and discipline in childrearing. But parenting has to come from a place of love and respect, not control.

What does parental control look like? At the most prosaic end of the spectrum, it looks like not allowing children to do what they can for themselves in age-appropriate ways, sometimes because it's easier for the parents to do it themselves. (Think of the college student who has no idea how to do his laundry.) Or not allowing them to have choice occasionally, in age-appropriate ways (milk or juice?). Worse is putting them down verbally, making fun of them, which is a form of punishment that manipulates them to seek approval—a form of reward. Or expecting them to satisfy adult emotional needs, instead of caring about satisfying theirs. When I was a child, my mother forced me to sit on the porch next to her and watch other children play. Apparently, she wanted to exercise control of me and/or have some company more than she wanted me to have a good time. The most extreme and heartbreaking examples make headlines: the parents whose need to control is so

Ernie   Prior to beginning my step journey, I was consumed with fear, doubt, and insecurity, though I could hardly understand how those concepts actually operated within me and my life. When I began the work, I had little understanding of myself beyond the notion that I could not drink safely.

Joan   On the outside, I appeared to have everything a twenty-one-year-old could ever want. On the inside, I was falling apart. At school and work I was full of fear and insecurity—I wasn't as smart as my classmates or co-workers, or as sophisticated or as funny . . . The list goes on and on. Despite the fear, I excelled both academically and professionally, although I certainly did not enjoy it. Drinking and smoking helped me relax and let go of some of my fears.

In my twenties and into my early thirties, I achieved much success in my career and my personal life, yet at times I was very unhappy. I didn't know who I was, what I valued, or what I wanted.

At my first AA meeting I immediately identified with the speakers, especially when they talked about "unfounded, ungrounded fear." My life was chaotic even when I wasn't drinking. I felt like I was on a treadmill and couldn't get off. I was so caught up in the planning, analyzing, and critiquing of everything and everyone around me that I wasn't enjoying my life. My life had become unmanageable because I was trying to control everyone and everything. It was simply exhausting.

out of control that they lock their child in a closet and virtually starve him.

Most of us never learn how to meet our own needs, only how to use other people—and further, anything outside ourselves—to get them met. We ourselves manipulate and control, reward and punish, as our parents manipulated and controlled, rewarded and punished us. An apt way to put it is that we develop a *using* mentality.

If you look carefully at your life, you'll probably begin to see, as I did, that every relationship you have ever known, whether to a person, a thing, or a substance, has been a rerun of this deeply conditioned dynamic. It is the only model many of us have for relating to the world. Oftentimes my clients come to me with no idea of what they really want, of what is good for them. And what if they did know? They have no sense of their own power to get what they need, to give to themselves, to love themselves.

Fear, Control, and Manipulation

What happens when you are emotionally dependent in this way? How does it play out?

First, to be emotionally dependent is to be afraid. What else can you be when, deep down, you believe that you can't help yourself but must instead rely on others for your survival? It is an encompassing fear that you will lose what you think you have or not get what you need or want. (I first ran across this notion of fear in AA's *Twelve Steps and Twelve Traditions,* Step 7.) It can manifest as a general anxiety, or as quite specific fears. *What will I do if I lose this job? What if she won't marry me? What if he leaves me? What if I get sick? What if I get fat? What if I can never lose this weight? What if I don't succeed? What if . . . ?*

Relapse begins here. This fear, in turn, triggers conscious or unconscious attempts to control and manipulate—others, yourself, substances—the goal being to fill the need. *How can I fix it? What can I say? What can I do to make him love me? What can I do to get my way?* The subsequent behaviors are endlessly inventive. They may involve rewards or punishments, or they may be less directly manipulative. They can be as extreme as stalking a girlfriend, starving yourself, or getting sick to elicit sympathy, or as subtle as telling a white lie or speaking very softly (a way to manipulate people into giving you their attention, as is yelling). Yes, all these attempts to control and manipulate others are symptoms of emotional dependency.

But the strategy of control and manipulation can only fail. Ultimately, we are all powerless over everything outside ourselves, are we not? We can't control what other people do or feel, we can't control events. And so the fear, control, and manipulation perpetuate themselves and progressively worsen. We don't get what we want, we still aren't happy, so we become yet more fearful and desperate, more controlling and manipulative.

When you continually look outside yourself to meet your needs, you may become dependent on a specific "other," be it a person, situation, or thing. On the deep level at which the conditioning of emotional dependency took place, you believe that you need . . . insert your addiction here . . . to survive. So when the object of your dependency is withdrawn or is threatened to be, fear, control, and manipulation become even more intense, in proportion to the intensity of the dependency. Anxiety turns to dread; dread turns to panic; pleas escalate to threats and finally to violence. Drinking a little becomes drinking a lot becomes drinking yourself into the gutter or into an early grave.

All of this is reenactment of the parent-child dynamic, but it can simultaneously be simple pain relief. When our control efforts fail, as they must, we feel not only fear but also pain. Some of us will reach for a drink or other drug, legal or illegal. Others for a slice of cake (or the whole thing), a sexual encounter, a roll of the dice, more time at work, a new outfit, a new relationship, more exercise, more therapy, more twelve-step meetings, more, more, more . . . And so the behavior both perpetuates and temporarily alleviates, or at least distracts us from, our pain. A vicious circle within the vicious circle. Talk about a trap.

This complex of fear, control, and manipulation—a survival mechanism at heart—is the hallmark of addiction. It's the way of life that lands people like you and me in twelve-step programs.

Love

You may be having a hard time reconciling the picture I've drawn of parenting and the damage it does with the belief—the certainty!—that parenting is about love. Especially if you are a parent working hard to do a good job. We love our children . . . don't we? I asked myself that question as I was learning all this. The answer is, we try. We really do. But many of us don't know much about love. Our parents were too caught up in the emotional dependency they learned from their own parents; we in turn are too caught up in the emotional dependency we learned from them; and so it will be for our own children if we do not break the cycle.

Consequently, the majority of parents use not only other adults but also their children to meet their emotional needs. How many times have you heard a mother say, "I wanted a baby to love who would love me back, love me forever." The problem is that she herself has not experienced love. She may even recognize this and be determined to give her child all the love she did not get. But you cannot give what you do not have.

Once again, I speak from experience. I had no idea how to be a good parent when I held my first child in my arms. I simply felt joy. There were people around me who could teach me how to meet the physical needs of an infant, but I came to the most important role of my life from a place of profound ignorance, totally unprepared. As I grew to understand the extent of my own emotional dependency, I had to admit that despite my best intentions, despite studying all the "right" parenting books, all I had to give my children was what my parents had given me: a survival mechanism designed to get my own needs met. By then I was in my fifties, but I finally began to learn to meet my own emotional needs, and thereby to *love* my children, not just need them. When I think of all that lost time . . . What a pity, for them and for me. But it is never too late to change and to heal.

I would not describe this missing love as "unconditional love."

Paul   I started drinking at a young age and drank as much as I could as often as I could. I started using other drugs soon after that. By my mid-teens, I was using heroin now and then. I never snorted it. I always shot it.

At one time I had my own home, was married with two children, had two cars, two cats, a respected construction company, many friends, and a serious drinking problem. Six years later, my home had been taken by the bank. My wife had left me and filed for divorce. The kids were gone with her, terrified and confused. The construction company was in bankruptcy court. I had no friends. I had two DWIs. I had been in jail twice, more than a year total. I had no job. I had no place to sleep or wash. I was sometimes suicidal. I hated everyone, but especially myself.

Eight years passed, and I still had no place to stay. I was doing small jobs for carpenters when I could. I had six DWIs and had been in jail six times, for a total of over three years. I had seen my kids, very briefly, no more than ten times. We had no relationship. I had been in and out of detoxes, thirty-day programs, and halfway houses for three years. I didn't understand anyone or anything in AA or NA.

Carolena From the outside, it looked like I had it all, but inside I was a frightened, insecure, bitter woman. I didn't need a drink, I didn't do drugs, I didn't eat to comfort myself, and I didn't gamble, not even the lottery. But I had been searching for my authentic self for a long time, a spiritual self. I had no sense of self and I was truly lost. I was always looking outside myself for love, happiness, approval, acknowledgement . . . surely someone or the next thing would eventually provide it. The opinions of others mattered a great deal to me, certainly more than my own.

I had been married for thirteen years. My anger and resentment were growing inside me, and unfortunately I was taking them out on my husband. I was mad if he helped and I was mad if he didn't help. I asked his opinion and then was mad at the opinion he gave me. I was mad because he wasn't reading my mind. I felt like I was being pulled in a million different directions and that the world did not value me. I was turning into my mother—there was always this underlying tension around her, you could feel it.

I was seriously considering therapy again. But I hesitated because I had done it in the past and, in the end, it didn't help that much, if at all.

That phrase implies that there is some form of love that can be conditional. Love is love. It is a gift. If something is expected in return, it is not love but rather a manipulation aimed at getting someone to meet needs that you are meant to meet for yourself.

So what would truly loving parenting look like? That topic merits a whole book. In short, though, it would be child-centered, not self-centered. It would encourage healthy independence, not dependence. It would recognize that children need nurturing, not obedience training. As Elisabeth Kübler-Ross put it in a letter to me, we would raise our children in "a natural, not normal, way."[10]

Dr. Maria Montessori, the physician, professor, intellectual, and edu-

---

[10] Dr. Elisabeth Kübler-Ross, personal letter to Dr. Rosemary Brown (30 Aug. 1991).

cator, recognized all this and put it to work in the classroom, through what came to be known as the Montessori Method of education. She found that children do not need discipline to learn, but are self-disciplined when offered some structure and age-appropriate tools. Once absorbed in an activity, a child is no different from an adult who is absorbed in a project and never thinks to watch the clock. Children don't need stars or criticism; they intuitively know when they've done a great job. They have a love of beauty, are compassionate toward their peers, and grow creatively when their individual gifts are encouraged. All this is equally applicable to parenting, which is the most important form of teaching.

Montessori also recognized that a child is, first and foremost, a spiritual being, precious and deserving of all good. The spirit is nurtured through a harmonious environment, and by being surrounded by people who are affectionate and loving, who give to us just because we are here, not because they want something from us.

The Indian-born spiritual thinker and teacher J. Krishnamurti considered the question of parental love:

> What does it mean to love a child? Surely, it does not mean encouraging him to become your little image, shaped by society, by so-called culture; it means, rather, helping him to grow freely. . . . to love him is to help him from the beginning to free himself constantly, so that he becomes a real individual, not merely an imitative machine.[11]

That all sounds wonderful, doesn't it? Alas, we do not yet have a parenting system that is truly child-centered, that creates free and independent individuals. And even if it appeared out of thin air, right now, it would be too late for you and me. No, we must do the work of freeing ourselves.

• • • • •

And so I came to understand that emotional dependency was learned. That meant it could be unlearned. People like me had to incorporate into their being a new model for relating to the world. Until we did that, no

---

[11] J. Krishnamurti Online, "Talks by Krishnamurti in India 1955–1956 (Verbatim Report) Banaras, Madras, Madanapalle, Bombay" (sixth talk in Bombay, 21 Mar. 1956): accessed 18 Jul. 2014, http://www.jkrishnamurti.org/krishnamurti-teachings/view-text.php?tid=541&chid=4860&w=21%20march%201956.

matter how much information we had about the problem, we would suffer its symptoms—addictive behavior in all its forms. We could abstain from our drug of choice for decades, and still we would suffer.

When I came to these realizations, I was very excited. I saw how the trap was built. The conventional wisdom was and is that addictions arise from multiple causes and are therefore complex to treat. But if every addiction served the same function and arose from the same cause, then it stood to reason that all could be addressed with the same treatment.

It would take years of trial and error, but I eventually arrived at the unique method of working the Twelve Steps that is outlined in this book, including the Fourth Step Algorithm. It's more accurately called a process than a treatment: learning is a process, not an event, and so is unlearning. It worked for me. It has worked for my clients and sponsees. It can work for you. It heals addictive behavior because it enables you to incorporate into your being a new model of emotional *independence*. It frees your mind and spirit from most of the childhood and other conditioning that prevented you from ever knowing the real meaning of love, from ever loving yourself, from ever becoming a truly autonomous individual. It is a way out of the trap and into the life you were meant to live.

Key Concepts

Control The goal of parenting as most of us know it. Control over a child is established by cultivating emotional dependency through the manipulation of rewards and punishments.

Fear, control, and manipulation This complex, at heart a survival mechanism, is the result of emotional dependency. The fear that we will not get what we think we need or want triggers control and manipulation of "the other" (person, substance, or situation)—i.e., addictive behavior—in an attempt to get it.

Love Love is love. It has no opposite. If it's "conditional," it's not love; it's control and manipulation.

Chapter 4

A Spiritual Solution

His craving . . . was the equivalent, on a low level, of the spiritual thirst of our being for wholeness, expressed in medieval language: the union with God.

—Carl Jung
The Bill W. and Carl Jung letters

If we were loved as children, I don't think we would feel a spiritual deficit. But we weren't, and we do. We thirst for the love we deserved but were denied. And what is God if not love? "Whoever does not love does not know God, because God is love," as the Bible's John 4:8 says (King James version). Dr. Jung was talking about alcohol, but I suspect he would agree that all addictions reflect the thirst for this love—for wholeness, as he put it, for union with God. I should say, union with "God" (we'll come back to that).

Bill and Carl

In AA circles, alcoholism is often referred to as a "spiritual disease." Indeed, Alcoholics Anonymous, to its great credit, has recognized the spiritual component of addiction from the beginning—with some help from Jung, as documented in an exchange of letters between Jung and AA cofounder Bill Wilson (Bill W., in the first-names-only tradition of AA) just months before Jung's death.

The initial letter from Bill to Jung in Zurich is dated January 23, 1961. He introduces himself as a cofounder of the society of Alcoholics Anonymous and then refers to a conversation Jung had with an alcoholic patient, Roland H., that had played a critical role in the founding of AA in 1935. After a year under Jung's care, Roland had moved on, full of confidence. But he soon relapsed and returned. Bill writes that Roland had told him of the celebrated psychiatrist's frank advice: further medical or psychiatric treatment was useless, and the only hope lay in a spiritual or religious experience. "This candid and humble statement of yours," Bill writes, "was beyond doubt the first foundation stone upon which our society has since been built." Bill goes on to describe his own spiritual recovery from alcoholism and how AA came into being, and thanks Jung for his unknowing role.[12]

Jung's January 30, 1961, response is even more interesting. He reveals to Bill that he hadn't told Roland everything he'd wanted to, because "in those days" he had to be careful of what he said due to being constantly "misunderstood in every possible way." At stake then was his scientific reputation. He had a medical degree and considered himself to be a scientist, yet he had a deep interest in spirituality and saw the human psyche as religious by nature.

> . . . Thus I was very careful when I talked to Roland H. But what I really thought about, was the result of many experiences with men of his kind.
>
> His craving for alcohol was the equivalent, on a low level, of the spiritual thirst of our being for wholeness, expressed in medieval language: the union with God.*
>
> How could one formulate such an insight in a language that is not misunderstood in our days?
>
> The only right and legitimate way to such an experience is that it happens to you in reality and it can only happen to you when you walk on a path which leads you to higher understanding. You might be led to that goal through an act of grace or through a personal and honest contact with friends, or through a higher education of the mind beyond the confines of mere rationalism. . . .
>
> I am strongly convinced that the evil principle prevailing in this world leads the unrecognized spiritual need into perdition, if it is not counteracted either by real religious insight or by the protective wall of human community.

With the asterisk, he refers to Psalm 42.2: "As the hart panteth after the water brooks, so panteth my soul after thee, O God."

---

[12] AA *Grapevine*, Jan. 1963: accessed 18 Jul. 2014, http://www.silkworth.net/ pdf BillW/The-Bill-W-Carl-Jung-Letters-Jan-1963.pdf.

Jung closes by noting that *alcohol* in Latin is *spiritus,* or "spirits": "You use the same word for the highest religious experience as well as for the most depraving poison. The helpful formula therefore is: *spiritus contra spiritum.*" That is, "spirituality against spirits."

I understand Jung's caution. A half century later, talking about spirituality and addiction still invites suspicion or ridicule. To begin with, the word *spiritual* is usually equated with *religion* and is often used synonymously. So the concept of addiction as a spiritual disease is quickly disregarded by anyone opposed to religious dogma and institutions. That's a mistake, if an understandable one. It is almost impossible to describe spirituality; it is limitless, while language is bounded, not to mention freighted with cultural baggage. Still, I'll try to tell you what I'm talking about when I say *spiritual,* because it is through a spiritual life—and even an atheist can have one—that you will quench the thirst that drives your addiction.

A Spiritual Life

First, let's talk about what spirituality is *not.* It is not religion. For good reason, the formal definition of *religion,* in my dictionary at least, does not even include the word *spirit. Religion* refers to a "personal set or institutionalized system of . . . attitudes, beliefs, and practices,"[13] or to a commitment to such a system. Any given religious system may or may not promote spirituality, but even if it does, it is not the thing itself. Many of us grew up with religion and have rejected it as damaging to us, or at least disappointing. Just think about some of the words associated with religion: *rules, regulations, rituals, hell, punishment, damnation, sin, dogma, obedience, holy.* For years I thought of myself as an atheist. I'd had enough of the God, or rather the religion, in which I was raised.

And what *is* spirituality? It's taken me a lifetime to answer that question for myself. I define *spirit* as that which is life giving, that which promotes wholeness, not holiness. The philosopher Spinoza said that if God is infinite—as almost any notion of God would have it—then

---

[13] *Merriam-Webster's Collegiate Dictionary,* 11th Edition (Springfield, MA, 2004), 1051.

nothing is outside of God.[14] We are all parts of the whole. There is no "other"; "God" is you.

It may be accurate to define God as love, but this is not necessarily helpful for the spiritual seeker when you consider that most people have never really experienced love or learned how to love themselves. Again, what we call love is, for the most part, control and manipulation—the model we learned from our parents, and they from theirs. (Thus the dilemma presented by Christ's commandment to "love thy neighbor as thyself"—that's exactly what we do.) When I first started in AA, the only way I could begin to grasp the concept of God was to substitute the word *good*. I had learned that the old Saxon word for *good* is spelled *g-o-d,* and that Plato, in his "Allegory of the Cave," describes "the Good" as "the cause of all that is correct and beautiful in anything."[15] It seemed possible for me to love good with my whole being. And I found that, indeed, a spiritual life could consist of finding and cultivating the "God" or "good" within me, which had been suffocating under the conditioning of child-hood and beyond, under all the ideas and beliefs and behaviors that had divorced me from my true and good self—from God. There was nothing wrong with me. And there is nothing wrong with you. I'm going to say that again: there is nothing wrong with you, with your good and true self. What's wrong is all the garbage piled on top of you.

It's often said that hell is the absence of God, which I take to mean separation from the God within. If you are addicted, you know hell very well, don't you? You are walled off, from yourself, from everyone, from everything. Walled in, by a consciousness bent on self-destruction. How do you achieve the union with God, the wholeness, that is your birthright and your true craving? For most people, it's hard to know where to begin. Few of us have been given a foundation for a spiritual life. But this is precisely what the Twelve Steps can provide.

If you are familiar with twelve-step programs, this idea may surprise you. It has been over forty years since I returned to AA, and in all those years I have never heard anyone talk about going to AA or any other step group for a spiritual life. We go because it is the only place

---

[14] *Stanford Encyclopedia of Philosophy,* http://plato.stanford.edu/entries/spinoza, accessed 18 Jul. 2014.

[15] Plato, *Republic,* Book 7, "The Allegory of the Cave," G.M.A. Grube and C.D.C. Reeve translation (Indianapolis: Hackett Publishing Co., 1992), 517.

Addiction Is the Symptom

left. Sometimes we are sent there by a court. We go because we think we may discover "from them" how to drink or eat or have sex normally and healthfully. We go to please people who have threatened to leave us if we don't stop whatever it is, or because, after trying to do it by ourselves—perhaps for years—we have failed. We may believe that God has failed us. The last thing we want to hear about is God.

As I hope you now see, though, a more spiritual approach to the Twelve Steps merely fulfills their original intention, as reflected in Bill W.'s correspondence with Jung. And if you call yourself an atheist, I hope you are at least beginning to see that rejecting religion doesn't have to mean rejecting the spiritual aspect of your being, which is yours alone to define.

In the coming chapters, you will learn how to work the steps in a way that not only fulfills their original intention, but also realizes their full potential as a spiritual practice that heals—that reunites you with the God within and cultivates the growth and deepening of that primary relationship for the rest of your life. Imagine your thirst for *more, more, more* . . . quenched, at last. As the French philosopher and social activist Simone Weil said, "If we go down into ourselves we find that we possess exactly what we desire."[16]

Key Concepts

Religion A system, whether personal or institutionalized, of attitudes, beliefs, and practices, or a commitment to such a system. Any given religious practice may or may not promote spirituality.

Spirituality Sensitivity to the spiritual, or a state of being spiritual. That which is spiritual is that which is life giving: that which promotes wholeness, not holiness.

God A concept you must ultimately define for yourself. But if God, also known as your higher power or higher self, is infinite, then nothing is outside of God, including you. No matter what you've done or failed to do.

---

[16] Simone Weil, *Gravity and Grace* (London/New York: Routledge Classics, 2002), 22.

Part 2

The Work

Chapter 5

The Twelve Steps, Revisited

To show others precisely how we have recovered is the main purpose of this book.

—Alcoholics Anonymous

You now understand the nature and cause of your addiction, as well as the nature of the solution. So it is time for me to share with you *precisely* how I and my many clients and sponsees healed ourselves of addiction—to drugs, food, work, relationships—with my approach to the Twelve Steps, and with the Fourth Step Algorithm in particular.

When I began my life in AA for the second time, on April 15, 1971, all I knew was that I did not want to drink again. Because that desire never left me, I persisted for decades in my search for a solution to relapse. As I've described, that search became increasingly systematic. Through my graduate work in the 1990s and then my private counseling practice, my understanding of the nature and cause of addiction grew, and I learned more about what worked and what didn't. I did not relapse. I went through chapter 5 of *Alcoholics Anonymous,* "How It Works," and "Step Four" in *Twelve Steps and Twelve Traditions* with a fine-tooth comb. Over the years, I shared my insights and my evolving modifications of the steps with hundreds of sponsees and clients, and I learned yet more from their experiences.

Eventually, it became clear that I had succeeded, even beyond what I set out to do. I had modified the steps in such a way that they did not merely prevent relapse into one's primary addiction—the symptom—but rather healed the emotional dependency that triggers all addictive behavior. While the traditional single-symptom approach virtually guarantees relapse of some kind, in my experience this new, all-inclusive step process offers a very real possibility of healing.

By now, you are coming to understand that my step method differs from the traditional one in important ways that include not only nuts and bolts, but also underlying premises. Before I discuss each step, let me summarize the seven key differences here. Keep them in mind if you are reading the Big Book or the *Twelve and Twelve*.

1. My method assumes that healing is possible. As the program would have it, you will always be "in recovery," never recovered. The labeling of a disease as "chronic" or "incurable" does not mean that it can't be healed, only that no one has yet figured out how to do it. As I've noted, the premise that addiction is chronic is based primarily on the high rate of relapse associated with traditionally available programs and therapies. In my experience, it can be healed through the modified step process outlined in this book.

2. My method focuses on cause rather than symptom. The Big Book's symptom focus is a fundamental error—and a primary cause of the high rate of relapse. The absurdity of focusing on symptoms is evident too in the ever-growing list of Twelve Step groups, one for every manifestation of addiction. My step method tackles the cause of these myriad addictive behaviors and thus can be effective for anyone, regardless of the form the addiction takes.

3. My method eliminates trial and error. One reason for the high rate of relapse, I believe, is the practice of doing the steps—in particular Step Four—by personal interpretation. My Fourth Step Algorithm comprises a set of practical, well-researched instructions that eliminate trial and error. It directly and thoroughly (but gently) addresses the fear, control, and manipulation that drive addictive behavior, with consistent results.

4. My method focuses on empowerment, not powerlessness. While I ask you to accept your powerlessness over *all of life,* not just your drug of choice, this acceptance is ultimately about recognizing, reclaiming, and acting on the power you *do* have.

5. My method focuses on the wrongs *you* have suffered. Traditionally, the Step Four inventory is largely a collection of the wrongs you've done. In my method, it is an inventory of the wrongs you yourself have suffered, including at your own hands. It reveals the lifetime of trauma that conditioned your addictive behavior—trauma being the result of any distressing experience, ranging from a disappointment to physical violence.

6. My method assumes your inherent goodness. The Big Book's premise is that you are flawed. It continually encourages self-judgment with such phrases as "flaws in our makeup," "character defects," and "spiritually sick." This is another fundamental error. My work assumes that it's not you who are defective, but rather the conditioning imposed on you.

7. My method utilizes professional help. Sponsorship can be extremely valuable. But I recommend that you choose a professional therapist or counselor to facilitate the step process outlined in this book. This process has powerful psychological components. The understanding, rigor, and insight of a talented, experienced professional will help ensure your success. This is discussed in more detail in chapter 8.

· · · · ·

Each step is discussed individually below, but it's helpful to think about them as falling into five groups, especially if you are new to the steps:

1. Steps One, Two, and Three The power steps. These concern the power you don't have, but also the power you do have, and its source. Taken together, these steps are truly your foundation for healing. I've made a key change to Step One: the condition of powerlessness applies not merely to your drug of choice, but to *all of life.*

2. Steps Four and Five The inventory steps. These steps are the core of my method and will take up the bulk of your time. The support of a qualified facilitator (see chapter 8) is indispensable. Again, there are two critical changes to Step Four: the inventory is not of yourself, but of *all your relationships,* and not of the ways you may have hurt others, but of the lifetime of trauma *you* have suffered.

3. Steps Six and Seven The "ready and willing" steps. These concern finding the willingness and humility to change, given all you've learned in the previous steps.

4. Steps Eight and Nine The amends steps. While the Fourth Step Algorithm focuses on the wrongs *you* have suffered, you still need to clear your history and your consciousness of any harm you may have caused.

5. Steps Ten, Eleven, and Twelve The maintenance steps. These define the steps as a practice, a way of life.

It takes most people three to eleven months to complete the steps as modified in this book. Ideally, you'll do all twelve in order with your facilitator. Professional support is most critical for Steps Four and Five. *These consciousness-changing steps are the focus of my step method and con-*

The Original Twelve Steps of Alcoholics Anonymous

1. We admitted we were powerless over alcohol—that our lives had become unmanageable.

2. Came to believe that a Power greater than ourselves could restore us to sanity.

3. Made a decision to turn our will and our lives over to the care of God as we understood Him.

4. Made a searching and fearless moral inventory of ourselves.

5. Admitted to God, to ourselves, and to another human being the exact nature of our wrongs.

6. Were entirely ready to have God remove all these defects of character.

7. Humbly asked Him to remove our shortcomings.

8. Made a list of all persons we had harmed, and became willing to make amends to them all.

9. Made direct amends to such people wherever possible, except when to do so would injure them or others.

10. Continued to take personal inventory and when we were wrong promptly admitted it.

11. Sought through prayer and meditation to improve our conscious contact with God as we understood Him, praying only for knowledge of His will for us and the power to carry that out.

12. Having had a spiritual awakening as the result of these steps, we tried to carry this message to alcoholics, and to practice these principles in all our affairs.

---

stitute the real "work." As such, they are explained in full detail in chapter 6.

Appendix A outlines the Brown Method, including the Fourth Step Algorithm. You may find it helpful to refer to it once you have read the book and are actually working through the steps.

Dr. Brown's Modified Twelve Steps

1. **We admitted we were powerless over life**—people, situations, circumstances, and substances—and that our lives and our minds were unmanageable when we tried to control any part of it.

2. Came to believe that a power greater than ourselves could help us **find sanity.**

3. Made a decision to turn over our will and our lives, **and the lives of others,** to the care of this power—the God of our understanding.

4. Made a searching and fearless moral inventory **of all relationships.**

5. Admitted to God, to ourselves, and to another human being the exact nature of our **relationships.**

6. Were entirely ready to **leave our defective conditioning behind.**

7. Humbly asked God to help us do this.

8. Made a list of all persons we had harmed, **including ourselves,** and became willing to make amends to them all.

9. Made direct amends to such people wherever possible, except when to do so would injure them or others.

10. Continued to take personal inventory and when we were wrong promptly admitted it.

11. Sought through prayer or meditation to improve our conscious contact with the God of our understanding, seeking only knowledge of God's will for us and the power to carry that out.

12. Having had a spiritual awakening as the result of these steps, we tried to carry this message to others and to practice these principles in all areas of our lives.

Step One: Accept Reality

We admitted we were powerless over life—
people, situations, circumstances, substances—
and that our lives and our minds were unmanageable
when we tried to control any part of it.

By the time you find yourself in a step program—or with a book like this in your hands—you are probably ready to admit that you are powerless over your addiction and that your life is unmanageable because of it. When I walked through the doors of AA for the first time, I know I was. By now, though, I hope you've come to understand that your primary addiction is not your fundamental problem, but rather a symptom of it. Consequently, there's an important change to this step: we admitted that we were powerless not over any single addiction, but over *life*. So revised, this step requires much more of us, and it gives much more as well.

Remember what you learned in chapter 3 about the roots of addiction: the obedience training that is parenting as most of us have known it creates emotional dependency; emotional dependency triggers addictive behavior; addictive behavior is characterized by a complex of fear, control, and manipulation. The key word here is *control*. Again, it's the original addiction. You can't control that which is outside yourself—what other people do or feel, situations, events. To think you can is the very definition of insanity. And so fear, control, and manipulation perpetuate themselves and progressively worsen. The first step out of this vicious circle is to recognize your powerlessness over *all of life*, not just over your drug of choice.

In this respect, the original Twelve Steps set you up for failure, meaning relapse. From the outset, you are focusing on the symptom— "powerless over X"—not the underlying control issues. Therefore you are likely doomed to drift from one twelve-step program to another as you engage in symptom substitution, or to give up in frustration because progress is so slow. As long as you are in a losing power struggle with everything and everyone around you, and as long as you are blaming anyone else for your misery, healing is impossible.

It is true that it is difficult to accept our fundamental powerlessness. (Steps Six and Seven speak to this, as does the mantra "Let go and let God.") Consequently, acceptance of our powerlessness is a life-

Jen   It is this issue of control that was integral to my recovery.
It was my belief that I had control over places, people, and
things that led to my resentments and hurts. I came to learn that I
have no control over anything or anyone except myself. This helps
me now when I get in a pinch, when I feel the resentments. Now I
look (with a clear mind, a sober mind) at why I'm feeling resent-
ful and/or hurt and understand that most likely I am attempting
to control someone or something other than myself, and I simply
have to "turn this over" and let it go!

long daily spiritual practice. Indeed, Step One, understood in the broad
way I've described, marked the beginning of my own spiritual life and
continues to be its foundation; after all these years, I still have control
issues. However, you can come very far, very fast. I've seen so many
clients do it. And the rewards are tremendous.

Once you recognize your powerlessness over other people and
things, you have taken the first step toward *personal* power, toward *self-*
control, toward restoring *choice*, toward healthy *independence*. In other
words, Step One, practiced in this way, is the beginning of the end of
emotional dependency, and thereby of addiction.

Step Two: Find Your Faith
Came to believe that a power greater than ourselves could help us find sanity.

Step Two, with its "power greater than ourselves," is an early stumbling
block for some people. If you haven't read chapter 4, "A Spiritual Solution," please do so. Still having trouble with the idea of a power greater
than yourself, within yourself? The simple bottom line is that you have
to accept that you're not in the driver's seat. You don't have to know
what is. After all, your spiritual journey is ahead of you, not behind
you. But coming to terms with this power, however vague your concept
of it may be, is prerequisite to your release from the *in*sanity of fear,
control, and manipulation.

Consider too that most of us, without recognizing it, believe in many *false* gods throughout our lives. Old words for God, cross-culturally, typically translate as "what is worshipped" and "the one sacrificed to." Our first gods are our parents. Then come other people, work, religion, sex, science, education, chemicals, food, and of course money (the church of commercialism is the most prosperous today). Your god is whatever you've exalted, been afraid to lose, sacrificed choice for, given your power to . . . only to get insanity in return. Why not give that power, that authority, to the God, or "good," within you?

It may be hard for you to believe—especially if you're an active chemical user—that such a "good" exists in yourself. You may be in quite a sorry state, full of self-loathing and remorse for the things you've done. But your "good" is there. Have some faith. Yes, *faith*. Another troublesome word for some of us. But all you have is faith of one kind or another. Fear is faith in negativity. Optimism is faith in positivity, a sense that good exists and will prevail. Why not choose to believe in positivity?

We often hear that seeing is believing. However, it is equally if not more true that we see what we believe. Our brains tend to reject, often without our realizing it, that which conflicts with our beliefs, whether those beliefs are conscious or unconscious. We literally don't take in the conflicting information. This phenomenon is called confirmation bias. It's a mental shortcut with profound consequences. The thoughts and beliefs that we consciously and unconsciously hold determine what we see—our experience of reality. And it is out of this "reality" that we create our lives.

The form of faith you have is a choice. And experience is—not always, but often—faith realized.

With regard to sanity, AA defines *in*sanity as doing the same thing over and over again while expecting different results. That's a good start. But as noted under Step One above, within the context of addictive behavior, it is more specifically and usefully defined as the continual attempt to control that which cannot be controlled and, further, to get your needs met through control and manipulation of externals.

I want to note too the subtle change in this step from "could restore us to sanity" to "could help us find sanity." You cannot be "restored" to sanity when in all likelihood you have never experienced it.

Our training in emotional dependency, and therefore our need for the illusion of control and our descent into the insanity of fear, control, and manipulation, starts earlier than we can even remember. Mere abstinence will not undo that training. But while you cannot be restored to sanity, you can *learn* it—by doing the work of this modified twelve-step process.

Step Three: Let Go
Made a decision to turn over our will and our lives, and the lives of others, to the care of this power— the God of our understanding.

Many years ago in an AA meeting, the group was discussing Step Three, and a hand went up. When the person was recognized, he said, "Having been raised a devout Catholic, how could I possibly know a God of my own understanding?" We all laughed, because no matter the denomination in which we had been trained, all that any of us had to rely on was dogma. Man-made rules and regulations, someone else's understanding. It was a continuation of the authoritarian childhood we had all experienced. And obviously, it didn't work, or we would not be sitting in an AA meeting.

Who can imagine turning one's will over to the God so many of us were raised with? The one who was keeping score of all the things we did wrong, the one who would punish us one way or another for acting like human beings instead of divine beings? That's not the God Step Three is talking about, or has ever talked about. Again, go back to chapter 4 if you need to. This is a spiritual process, not a religious one, and *this* step is wide open to personal interpretation.

Note my addition of "the lives of others" to the wording of this step. I know I'm not the only one who finds "turning over" my own life easier than turning over the lives of others—in particular, of those close to me. That difficulty may masquerade as concern, but too often it is about wanting others to want what we want for them. In other words, it's about control.

What kind of God do you want in your life? Imagine having a power in your life to guide, sustain, and comfort you just because you are here, a power that loves you just as you are. Why can't such a power be a part of the perfect you? The perfect you, the whole (not holy) you, that is untouched by all the conditioning that has made you less than perfect? This is the power, in whatever form it takes, that you need to believe in. It is this power that activates your ability to learn how to love yourself.

Consequently, Step Three can be seen as the beginning of self-parenting—of giving yourself the love you did not get from your parents. Another way to describe this is *dependency transformation*: a shift *from* dependency on a traditional God, on your own power, on other people, places, situations, and things, none of which provided what you needed, *to* dependency on a power greater than yourself, within yourself. The outcome of this transformation is a very different way of life: one of self-sufficiency and its accompanying empowerment, as opposed to other-dependency and its accompanying powerlessness.

Step Four: Take Inventory
Made a searching and fearless moral inventory of all relationships.

Once you understand the power you have and the power you don't, you are ready for Step Four, the most intensive of all the steps. Along with the associated fifth step, it is the focus of my step method. The AA texts offer a great deal of material on the step—there are more than four dozen directives and questions in chapter 5 of the Big Book and "Step Four" in *Twelve Steps and Twelve Traditions*—but little guidance for actually doing it. So as you may already have experienced, Step Four is typically a source of confusion and difficulty. Apparently, this has always been true. As far back as 1959, one researcher reported the following:

> The leaders of A.A. with whom I spoke specified that the largest percentage of those who had regressed into acute alcoholism were individuals who had stumbled in taking what is known as "step four" of the A.A. program, which involves "taking a moral inventory" and attempts toward self-analysis of themselves. In attempting such a self-evaluation outside of a therapeutic relationship, these alcoholics had become anxious and acted out by drinking again.[17]

---

[17] Hendrik Lindt, "The Rescue Fantasy in Group Treatment of Alcoholics," *Journal of Group Psychotherapy,* vol. 9 (Jan. 1959): 43–52.

Give yourself the credit you deserve for any and all previous attempts you have made to do this step.

My Fourth Step Algorithm is designed to address the factors that I believe have made the step a stumbling block, turning it instead into a tool for transformation. I'll explain the actual workings of the algorithm in the next chapter, but let's go over its meaning and intent here with the others.

No More Trial and Error

One thing that makes Step Four such a minefield is the practice of doing it by personal interpretation, i.e., by trial and error. The very control issues that drive addictive behavior are responsible for the prevailing understanding in the program that no one can tell you how to do this step, or any other for that matter. They can suggest, but not tell. Consequently, everyone muddles through, often going from one person to the next in search of suggestions. While you might luck out and find relief from your primary symptom, you won't heal the cause: the underlying control issues. The result is relapse, if not into your primary addiction, into a substitute that may be equally or more dangerous.

In this book, I am offering a set of practical, time-tested instructions, for Step Four in particular, that directly address your control issues and whose consistent result *when precisely followed* is healing.

Your Emotional History

Another problem with the traditional approach to Step Four is its focus on the wrongs you've done. Who wouldn't "become anxious and act out"? The Fourth Step Algorithm turns this old approach on its head by exploring every relationship in which *you* have been emotionally hurt—including your relationship with yourself—as far back as you can remember. Thus I've changed the wording from "made a searching and fearless moral inventory of *ourselves*" to "made a searching and fearless moral inventory of *all relationships*." Let me repeat, it's not about how you may have hurt others, but about the lifetime of hurts *you yourself* have suffered.

Through a literal inventory—a handwritten list—of all your relationships, you will gain a comprehensive view of your emotional history. This may sound daunting, but all you're really doing is spending

> **Ernie** Dr. Brown's method removed the element of trial and error. There was no room for my personal interpretations of my inventory items to cloud or encumber the work. Perhaps most valuably, her method and her focus on the fourth step inventory increased my understanding of the core causes of addiction. I was able to identify the fear, control, and manipulation that had defined my personal and professional relationships before I completed my step work.

twenty to thirty minutes a day making a list. Your facilitator will help you keep on track. That usually means checking in with him or her daily by phone, Skype, email, or text. Most people find that as they write, they become conscious of all kinds of stored, seemingly forgotten incidents whose residual effects are still shaping their lives.

Memory by memory, line by written line, you will begin to see how you were conditioned into fear and how (once you were old enough to make choices for yourself) you designed ways to control and manipulate people, substances, and situations to meet your needs. You will begin to see how all of this shaped and continues to shape your relationships. That is, you will become acutely aware of a lifetime of emotional trauma and addictive behavior. Simultaneously, the process begins to expose the part you've played in creating the majority of these hurtful experiences. With this awareness comes the ability to choose different behaviors.

Expectations and Resentments

A key emotion that you'll become more aware of, and then shed, through this inventory is resentment. A resentment is any emotional trauma, real or imaginary, that is not only "re-sent" in consciousness but also re-felt (the Old French *sentir* means to feel), through rumination or conversation. If you carry resentment, you are persistently steeped in indignation, blaming, and ill will. "Resentment is the number one offender," reads *Alcoholics Anonymous* at the beginning of this step. "It destroys more alcoholics than anything else" (page 64). That is quite true in my experience, although I would replace "alcoholics" with "people."

I would also replace *resentment* with *unfulfilled expectation*. In my copy of *Alcoholics Anonymous,* I long ago crossed out the one and wrote in the other. Indignation, blaming, and ill will certainly describe resentment, but a resentment is, at heart, an unfulfilled expectation. You don't get the former without the latter. You expect someone to do or be something, and he can't or won't. You expect a situation to turn out a certain way, and it doesn't. A promise is made, and it is not kept. You want to hear "yes," and you get "no." It hurts. It's disappointing. The hurt begins in childhood, and the disappointments pile up. Disappointments quickly turn to resentments as you replay them mentally and verbally, feeding yourself a never-ending tape of trauma to the soul. Consequently, it is impossible to heal your addiction until you deal with old resentments once and for all—and prevent the accumulation of new ones. You'll deal with the old ones in Step Four. How do you prevent new ones? By letting go of expectations.

"But isn't it normal to have expectations?" you might ask. Yes, in that they are as "normal" as addiction. Expectations occur in direct proportion to your dependency on others to fulfill your needs and wants, and dependency triggers fear, control, and manipulation—addictive behaviors.

Most of us never got the message that we are meant to fulfill our needs and wants ourselves; as discussed in chapter 3, the cultivation of dependency is the rule. Like addiction itself, expectations exist on a spectrum, and certainly some are less problematic than others. But in my experience even seemingly innocuous expectations set us up for disappointment and resentment. I suppose you can have as many expectations as you want, just so long as you are prepared to be disappointed (always have a plan B, even C). Because one thing I know for sure is that people and situations are unreliable. Whenever people tell me they are going to do something (or not do something), I try to take it not with a grain of salt, but with a pound. The problem we all face is that we believe what we are told because it is what we want to hear. That is, our expectations are based on wishful thinking, not reality.

Another thing I know for sure is that we must learn how to love ourselves enough that no matter what someone else does or doesn't do, says or doesn't say, we do not imagine that it reflects on us and are not too upset or disappointed.

Beyond merely letting go of expectations, you can actually come to experience so-called disappointments as gifts. Take "no," for example. When people say no to you, whatever the context, you can be grateful for their honesty (and if the tables are turned, they for yours). Imagine the potential for complications, including misplaced resentment toward *you,* if someone agrees to something unpalatable or not quite right. You can probably recall at least a few instances in which "no" saved you: "It's a good thing I didn't get that job"; "Thank God she didn't marry me." With practice, you can experience that gratitude sooner rather than later. Every time you get a no, rather than pressing for what, in that moment, you think you want, say (in your mind if not aloud), "Thank you." Smile and walk away, looking forward to what's to come instead.

One last point about resentment: If you understand the concept of a spirit-mind-body connection at all, it's no leap to see the correlation between resentment and illness of all kinds. Dr. John Sarno describes this phenomenon at length in his book *The Mindbody Prescription.* Among my clients, a common "side effect" of working through Steps Four and Five in particular is a return to physical health.

Beliefs and "Morals"

Another important outcome of the Fourth Step Algorithm is awareness of the beliefs that may be fueling your behavior—and the resulting ability to choose different ones. If you have never before examined your belief system, this step becomes an exercise in distinguishing your own truth from the beliefs fed to you in childhood, beliefs that you may have tried to follow but that produced only failure, guilt, and excruciating emotional, and oftentimes accompanying physical, pain. A recipe for addiction.

Which brings us to this step's sticky word, *moral,* one's morals being a set of beliefs concerning "ethical" or "right" behavior. For many people, the word has religious implications and therefore becomes a new stumbling block. In this context, the appropriate definition of right behavior is whatever is good for your *morale,* or sense of well-being. This is a personal judgment call that has little or nothing to do with whatever collective theory of right and wrong you may have learned. I've found this definition from Dan Custer's *The Miracle of Mind Power* useful:

> That is moral which is good for you—that which contributes to your greatest good. There is no moral law aside from the law of healthy expression; but your greatest good cannot be separated from your neighbor's greatest good. If you do not live up to that which you believe to be the greatest good, there is an inner mechanism of mind which causes you to be unhappy—which causes you pain. The inner instinctive mechanism is called conscience.[18]

Many of the moral principles that form your conscience are not eternal truths, but rather received "wisdom"—more externals that you've become dependent on. They may in fact not be moral. That is, they may not be good for you or those around you. Like so many of my clients, though, you may have no idea what *is* good for you. Most of us were not allowed to develop our identities as individuals. As discussed in chapter 3, from the time we were very young, our identities were forged by adults who wanted us to be mere images. Parents and other authority figures gave us the message, verbally and nonverbally, that to be different was to be wrong. So we learned to believe and want what we thought we were supposed to believe and want. Through the Fourth Step Algorithm, your own beliefs and desires are revealed—that is, your individual identity, along with your internal moral compass.

Freedom from Fear

As J. Krishnamurti wrote in his book *The First and Last Freedom,* "There can be freedom from fear only when there is self-knowledge. Self-knowledge is the beginning of wisdom, which is the ending of fear."[19] The self-knowledge that comes from doing the Fourth Step Algorithm eliminates a tremendous amount of fear. By the time my clients complete it, they understand, based on their own life experiences, that there is no need to be afraid or to attempt to control anyone or anything. Imagine no fear. Imagine even 50 percent less fear. Your suffering will end, but further, you will gain a practical sense of freedom you've probably never experienced.

---

[18] Dan Custer, *The Miracle of Mind Power* (Prentice Hall, 1991), 110–111.

[19] J. Krishnamurti, *The First and Last Freedom* (New York: Harper & Row, 1973), 11.

Step Five: Get Honest
Admitted to God, to ourselves, and to another human being the exact nature of our relationships.

As the companion to Step Four (and this too will be covered in more detail in the next chapter), Step Five should be done as soon as possible after you complete that step.

Step Five, done in person with your facilitator over one to three days, is an in-depth, intensive exploration of the incidents and feelings you uncovered and noted only briefly in Step Four. It may be the first time you've had a witness to validate the accumulated pain of these experiences. Your facilitator will also help you reinterpret your experiences via the lens of emotional dependency. And so it may also be the first time you've recognized your role in creating many of them.

Honesty

We begin our lives in honesty. We are taught to lie. Young children always tell the truth until they are punished for doing so, or until they realize that although adults talk about the importance of telling the truth, they in fact lie. Adolescents learn that circumstances, which adults attempt to control, dictate how and to what extent adults are willing to manipulate the truth, whether by omission or commission. This model is carried into adulthood.

The degree to which you lie and the degree to which you want things from others are directly related. That is, lying is another fear-driven attempt to control and manipulate—an addictive behavior. Even seemingly trivial lies can represent fear-driven attempts to manipulate

---

Jen | I was constantly on the lookout for someone finding out about me. I looked "normal" from the outside, but my whole life was centered around "fixing" what I had done while drinking, living with the shame, and continuing to promote the shame with my daily drunks. Living a life of shame and apologies is very different than living an honest, forward-moving life.

---

what others think of you. For example, you make up a story to explain why you didn't do something, when you just plain forgot. Or you say yes when you really want to say no, which, in addition to reflecting fear, promotes insanity.

Any addictive behavior promotes further addictive behavior, so the eventual outcome of lying can be the practice of multiple addictions. Healing, then, depends on being as honest as possible in all your affairs. At the same time, your honesty is a measure of your healing: honesty becomes possible when you are not driven by fear to attempt to control and manipulate people or situations with lies.

I don't remember exactly when I myself started lying, but without a doubt I was a liar by the time I got to AA. It's part of being addicted. When you can no longer control how much you're doing X, you start to hide how much you're doing it. The hiding itself is a kind of lie, and omissions and outright falsehoods are the necessary accompaniment. "How much do you drink?" your doctor asks. "Only one or two when I get home from work," you answer, leaving out that the glass is the size of a vase. If your problem is food, you eat in secret and may say—or even tell yourself—"It's genetic," or "It's my metabolism," or "I can't understand it. I eat so little." If you're in an abusive relationship, it's the same. The last thing you want anyone to know is that you made a mistake in your choice of partner, and that you stay despite the insults or bruises or broken bones. People who are addicted live in fear that someone will realize how bad off they are—and in even greater fear of realizing it for themselves. Thus we lie to ourselves as much as we lie to others.

The very idea that you have to get honest to recover may be terrifying. But by the time you finish this twelve-step process, you will find it much easier to practice honesty. You will have a stronger sense of identity. You will know, perhaps for the first time, who you are and what you want and do not want. You will have a desire and a willingness to provide for your own needs. All of this will empower you to practice honesty on a more constant basis in your relationships. You will also be motivated by a new understanding that once dishonesty comes into play and goes unchecked, relapse is imminent. Whether you realize it or not, the moment you want something from someone (a thing, an emotion, a circumstance, a substance), you slip into addictive mode. You begin to lie, to say or do whatever it takes to get your needs met. Honesty short-circuits all that. It's a natural boundary, the most effective tool I know for preventing or halting any addictive behavior. Notice that I say "practice honesty." It is a practice. You will probably be working on honesty for the rest of your life. But it gets easier. You may even have a few laughs about it along the way.

• • • • •

Once, when I was about eight years into the program, I lied to my son about receiving some Mother's Day flowers he'd asked his sister to pick up for me. She hadn't had time to do it, which she readily admitted to me. What was I to say when my son called that Sunday and said, "Happy Mother's Day! How are the flowers?" A simple question, a simple answer, you may think. However, my answer, while well intentioned, set in motion a series of events that illustrated the hazards of lying even in small ways.

I didn't want my son to be disappointed about my not getting the flowers, or disappointed in his sister, so I answered, "Oh thank you, they are beautiful. What a lovely present." Now, my son was away from home for an extended period for the first time, and he called most days just to check in. When he called the next night, he asked, "What does the bouquet look like, Mom?" It was the first time he hadn't been able to get me a Mother's Day present himself, so the bouquet had taken on undue importance. What could I do but describe the nonexistent flowers? The next day, though, before we hung up, he said, "You know, I wish so much I could see the bouquet. Will you send me a picture?"

By now I realized that I shouldn't have lied in the first place. What was I going to do? I was going to compound matters, of course. I called the florist, ordered a bouquet that fit the description I'd given my son, and picked it up on my lunch hour. When I got home, I took out my camera, set the bouquet in a bed of periwinkle in the front yard, leaned in to frame the shot . . . and burst into tears. I was taking a picture of a lie! I just couldn't do it.

Instead, I did what AA had taught me to do every time I lied: apologize and get on with life. I called my son that night in tears and told him what I had done. He said, "Oh Mom, that's okay. It bothers you because you hardly ever do it anymore." After we hung up, I thought,

"Yeah, it is okay. It wouldn't be okay if it hadn't bothered me."

And so it is that day by day, year by year, we learn the meaning of the "rigorous honesty" the program rightly calls for. The payoff is considerable. A consciousness that has no secrets is the first step toward gaining the freedom we need to create a healthy and satisfying life.

Personal Responsibility

As you share your fourth step inventory with your facilitator, you will begin to understand two things: the power of your thoughts and choice of words to determine how you experience any given incident, and how and why you may have co-created it, via thought or deed.

Just think how differently you might have experienced a given situation or relationship if you had not gone into it with expectations and then defined yourself as the wronged party when those expectations were not met. As I described under Step Four, expectations set you up for disappointment and therefore breed resentment. Also, by this point in the process you will have begun to see your own patterns of fear, control, and manipulation. A great deal of the emotional trauma you're carrying around may stem from these patterns, which continually get you into painful situations.

With these realizations comes a growing awareness of personal responsibility for refusing to act on addictive behaviors, lying among them. At first, you may catch yourself in the act and then stop; in time you will learn to dismiss the old behaviors as they surface in your consciousness. This is the very definition of healing within the context of addictive behavior: a qualitative change in consciousness that restores choice.

Between your facilitator's witnessing of your emotional history in Step Five and your awakening to your role in creating it, the emotional charge of it all is largely removed. You've cleaned house, taken everything out of storage and jettisoned it. However, the effect won't last if you keep feeding emotional energy into the past by thinking or talking about it.

Resentments die when they are not fed emotionally, and personal responsibility precludes resentment. If old resentments do come up, you can simply acknowledge them, be thankful they have been dealt with, and turn your thoughts to something else. As for new ones, you'll want to revisit the Fourth Step Algorithm at least annually, to get rid of any accumulations. Having been through the process before, you'll be able to do most of it on your own, with a sponsor instead of a professional serving as Step Five's witness if you wish.

The desire to control and manipulate people and situations to satisfy your own needs never goes away completely. However, once the Fourth Step Algorithm and Step Five show you the high cost of acting on that desire, you will no longer be willing to pay the price.

Step Six: Get Willing
Were entirely ready to leave our defective conditioning behind.

The "defects of character" referred to in this step's original wording can be summed up in one word: *control*. Remember Step One: the fantasy that you can control that which is outside yourself—what other people do or feel, situations, events—is a big part of your problem. To admit your powerlessness over *all of life* is to take the first step away from the vicious circle of fear, control, and manipulation that you were conditioned into as a child. But that admission, or recognition, is indeed only the first step. Step Six asks you to do something with that recognition. Are you ready and willing to stop your attempts to control and manipulate people, situations, circumstances, and substances?

Step Seven: Ask for Help
Humbly asked God to help us do this.

Once you are ready and willing to give up your attempts to control and manipulate externals, you'll need some help. It's fear that drives control, so in Step Seven you ask the God of your understanding to help you remove your fear whenever it surfaces. Once the fear is removed, so is the desire to control and manipulate. The humility required to ask for help can be learned. Humility is difficult for many people because they equate it with weakness. However, to be humble is simply to be teachable. The more you practice humility, the more willing you'll be to give up your desire to control everyone and everything around you. And the more you can do that, the more empowered you'll be to run your own life.

Paul   By my early thirties, I had come to the end of my rope. I was an empty shell. I shot five bags of heroin and woke up three days later in a motel room in a patch of dried-up vomit. That was the last time that I drank or took drugs.

That day, I ran into two men that I had met while in my last halfway house. They took me to an AA meeting. One of them told me he was my sponsor, and that night he told me to get on my knees and ask God for help. After he left, I reluctantly did as he had asked. I had tried to get sober many times. I don't think it's a coincidence that my obsession to drink and drug left me that night: for the first time in my life I had gotten on my knees and asked for help.

Step Eight: List Your Harms

Made a list of all persons we had harmed, including ourselves, and became willing to make amends to them all.

Steps Eight and Nine complete the self-assessment begun in Steps Four and Five. Having shared Step Four with another person in Step Five, you'll have the courage and fearlessness you need to complete these steps.

To make amends is to acknowledge and apologize for any harm you've caused another person—or yourself. It's another step toward taking responsibility for co-creating your life experiences. If you sincerely desire to clear away the wreckage of your past—in essence, your contribution to it—you will find the willingness you need to make amends.

Your list should include everyone, alive or dead, whom you have hurt. Your own name should be at the top of the list. You'll list anything you've done that could be considered hurtful, no matter how small. For example, although many people consider gossip to be just part of the human experience, in *Twelve Steps and Twelve Traditions* it is rightly referred to as character assassination. While you're thinking about character assassination, be sure to cover not only how you have talked about others, but also how you have talked to yourself about yourself—judging, criticizing, condemning.

Step Nine: Make Amends

**Made direct amends to such people wherever possible,
except when to do so would injure them or others.**

Step Nine opens an avenue for both settling past quarrels or differences with others and reconciliation with oneself. It allows for the possibility of forgiving ourselves and others.

Once again, you'll start with yourself. Some people find that they themselves are the main subject of Step Nine. Write a letter in which you apologize to yourself for all the pain you've caused yourself. It was all done in ignorance, but that doesn't mean it hurt any less. Itemize. List everything you did or did not do that was destructive to your well-being. End the letter by thanking yourself for all the *good* that you did or brought into your own life. Thanking yourself (and others, in your amends to them) completes the relationship cycle in a positive, affirming, and empowering way. Mail the letter to yourself, read it when it arrives, and then destroy it.

Make another list of the wrongs you have committed against others. It is important that your amends for these wrongs be made in person if at all possible. Ask each person to meet with you for a specific purpose—to handle old business—explaining that you are working on yourself and this is part of the process. If it is impossible to meet, or the person does not want to, then write a letter that covers everything you would have said.

This meeting is not a time for casual conversation that might cause you to deviate from the task at hand. Formal preparation will be helpful; be sure to have your list in front of you. Again, itemize: "1. I lied to you on _____ about _____. I know it was hurtful, and I want to apologize for that." Follow the wrongs with all that you have to be thankful for in the relationship.

At this moment, it may be difficult to imagine being thankful for *anything* in some of your relationships. Trust that by the time you have worked your way to Step Nine, you will be focusing on the good and will be able to find something, if only lessons learned.

Remember that it does not matter how your amend is received, only that you make it. In so doing, you're taking responsibility for your side of the relationship. As it says in the Big Book (page 83), "There may be some wrongs we can never fully right. We don't worry about them if we can honestly say to ourselves that we would right them if we could."

Note too that this process applies even to people who are deceased. If they are alive in your consciousness, amends need to be made. Make your lists as though you would be meeting with them. Then find a quiet, private place and speak to each of them as though they were in front of you, listening.

Once you have finished with the amends, when the incidents come to mind, dismiss them, feel grateful that you are finished with that phase of your life, and immediately turn your thoughts to something positive.

Taken together, Steps Four, Five, Eight, and Nine end the cycle of blaming others for our lives and the way we feel—and mark the beginning of acknowledging and assuming personal responsibility for our lives in the past, present, and future.

Step Ten: Stay Current
Continued to take personal inventory and when we were wrong promptly admitted it.

This is the "don't let the sun go down on your anger" step, the "one day at a time" step. As the Big Book notes (page 84), "Continue to watch for dishonesty, resentment, and fear." Or as I would say, more broadly, continue to watch for fear, control, and manipulation. This requires a daily inventory and daily amends.

If you lie, as soon as you become aware of it, apologize: "I don't know why, but I just lied about that." And keep in mind that dishonesty includes lying by omission. It is amazing how quickly you get out of the habit of lying when you find yourself apologizing constantly. The same goes for control and manipulation, which can be subtle. "I apologize for trying to persuade you [control you] to do thus and such."

Remember that your inventory includes any wrongs you have suffered—and recognition of the role you may have played, via any lingering emotional dependency, in creating the experience. If you have developed a resentment, you now realize that it stems from an unfulfilled expectation, and that expectation is a symptom of unhealthy dependency. You stop the dependency by recognizing that the problem is not what someone did or didn't do, but rather your response to it.

Fear leads to control and manipulation, so you must keep it in check. Ask for help—see Step Seven. Remember too that fear is simply faith in negativity; optimism is faith in positivity (see Step Two). Practice rejecting negativity and choosing positivity. You might be surprised by the result.

With practice, you will learn to refuse any form of fear, control, and manipulation as it surfaces—and thus heal your addictive behavior.

Step Eleven: Do Your Best

Sought through prayer or meditation to improve our conscious contact with the God of our understanding, seeking only knowledge of God's will for us and the power to carry that out.

Step Eleven is about developing a spiritual life, whatever that means for you. By the time you reach this step, you'll probably have some idea of what form that spiritual life might take. Just remember that it is yours and yours alone. You are allowed to make it up as you go along; let it evolve. My own very nourishing spiritual life is still on the move. It has been formed by a wide range of influences: the Bible, Unity, yoga, Krishnamurti, Buddhism, color therapy . . . I've done so much seeking, I'm not even sure how I acquired certain facets of my spiritual life, and that's fine.

Step Eleven of the Big Book (pages 85–88) provides an outline, a guide to beginning a spiritual practice. It includes contemplation each morning and a review of your day each night. Perhaps not all of it will resonate with you, but the part I think anyone can use successfully is this:

> We constantly remind ourselves we are no longer running the show, humbly saying to ourselves many times each day "Thy will be done." We are then in much less danger of excitement, fear, anger, worry, self-pity, or foolish decisions. We become much more efficient. We do not tire so easily, for we are not burning up energy foolishly as we did when we were trying to arrange life to suit ourselves.

At its heart, this step is a reminder that all we can do is our best, and the outcome will take care of itself.

Step Twelve: Help Others

Having had a spiritual awakening as the result of these steps, we tried to carry this message to others and to practice these principles in all areas of our lives.

Because my modified twelve-step process works equally well for all addictions (and because I don't like to label people with their addictions), I've changed Step Twelve from "carry this message to alcoholics" to "carry this message to others."

This step has three parts. First, it states that "a spiritual awakening has occurred as the result of these steps," the implication being that you must do all twelve. Second, those who have completed this process are expected to try to "carry this message," meaning the twelve-step process, to others. I'm working this piece of the step by writing this book. Finally, we are to "practice these principles in all our affairs," meaning work the steps as needed in daily life.

I can't emphasize the word *practice* enough. The Twelve Steps are the foundation for an ongoing spiritual practice. Step Twelve may be the last, but clearly it marks a beginning: the beginning of a new, conscious life.

Key Concepts

Algorithm A step-by-step procedure for solving any problem or achieving a certain end. A recipe is an algorithm. The Twelve Steps constitute an algorithm.

Powerlessness Ultimately, we are powerless over that which is outside ourselves. For this reason, the strategy of control and manipulation is a recipe for insanity. Recognizing this powerlessness (Step One) is the beginning of self-empowerment.

Faith You have faith in whatever you give your power to: people, things, ideas, situations, prejudices. Many of us give our power to fear, which is simply faith in negativity. Optimism is faith in positivity.

Moral In this context, whatever is good for your morale, or sense of well-being. Many of the moral principles that form your conscience are just more externals that you've become emotionally dependent on.

Honesty Lying is an addictive behavior—a manifestation of the complex of fear, control, and manipulation. All addictive behavior promotes further addictive behavior. We are dishonest in direct ratio to our emotional dependency.

Resentment An unfulfilled expectation. It occurs when your attempts to control and manipulate externals (people, substances, or situations) are frustrated.

Expectation You are powerless over anyone or anything but yourself, so to have expectations of other people, things, or situations is to invite resentment and therefore court fear, control, and manipulation—aka addictive behavior.

Insanity Within the context of addictive behavior, insanity can be defined as the belief that you have any control over that which is outside yourself. It's the continual attempt to get your needs met through control and manipulation of externals.

Sanity A learned state of mental soundness that includes the ability to anticipate and appraise the effects of your actions.

Chapter 6

The Fourth Step Algorithm

You must have a room, or a certain hour or so a day, where you don't know what was in the newspapers that morning, you don't know who your friends are, you don't know what you owe anybody, you don't know what anybody owes to you. This is a place where you can simply experience and bring forth what you are and what you might be. . . . At first you may find that nothing happens there. But if you have a sacred place and use it, something eventually will happen.

—Joseph Campbell
The Power of Myth

lgorithm. The word may be unfamiliar to you. I first encountered it when I started my graduate research and read about the importance of an "algorithmic" approach to problem solving in business and medicine. Narrowly defined, an algorithm is a step-by-step procedure for solving a mathematical problem. More broadly, it's a step-by-step procedure for solving any problem or achieving a certain end.

A recipe, for example, is an algorithm. To bake a cake successfully, you need to know not only the ingredients, but also what pan to use, the right oven temperature, the order in which to add the ingredients, how to combine them (stir, fold, whip?), how long to leave the cake in the oven, and what to do with it when you take it out (remove it from the pan? cool it first?). A single missing element can ruin the cake.

It occurred to me that the problem on which I was focused—relapse—needed an algorithm. The traditionally confounding fourth step was the obvious candidate.

The challenge in designing most algorithms is to define the algorithmic process in enough detail to work while making it easy to follow.

Paul Doing the fourth and fifth steps with Dr. Brown was the turning point of my sobriety and of my entire life. Up until that time, all I could remember hearing about the fourth step was that it was an insurmountable task. It was hard and emotionally draining and would take forever. Dr. Brown told me to treat it as a fact-finding mission. Every time I could come up with something that I had done in the past I would come to better know why I was and who I was now.

I had a hard time at first remembering anything at all from so long ago. It took weeks to write anything but the names of my family. But once I started to remember, I was off and writing. My fourth step flowed from me.

Patterns that had repeated themselves throughout my life came to light. I found that people, places, and institutions such as my boyhood religion had shaped me into who I am today. I remembered things that were done to me that hurt me so bad that I covered them up with drink and other drugs for years. Things that I had done to others and was so ashamed of that I couldn't have possibly thought about. I found that fear had ruled me throughout almost all of my life—getting worse as I got older. I wrote almost everything I could remember until I was nine or ten years old. From then on, I wrote down only pertinent things, or I would still be writing now.

Like any complex task, Step Four is far more readily understood and completed when broken into its component parts. I first extracted the useful directives and questions from the verbiage of the AA texts. Then, over the course of my work with hundreds of people over the years, I devised a straightforward seven-phase procedure for handling them in the context of my cause-focused approach. The resulting algorithm is indeed detailed and, despite the number of ingredients, easy to follow. And follow it you must, or you might not get the results you need and deserve.

Be prepared to spend several months on the seven phases of the Fourth Step Algorithm. It's not that much time when you consider the years many people spend in therapy, with unpredictable results. The more diligent you are, the sooner you'll finish and get on with your new life.

Preliminaries

Meeting with Your Facilitator

While most of the contact you need with your facilitator can be accomplished remotely, I recommend an in-person meeting at the beginning of the process. Your facilitator must be someone you like, and, in person, you'll more easily confirm that you have the needed rapport. But if the facilitator you want is far away, and you're willing and able to travel for Step Five—which absolutely must be done in person—don't let distance stop you. A long phone or Skype call is a good second choice for the initial meeting. I've had clients who were on the opposite coast. Chapter 8 discusses how to find a facilitator.

Again, ideally you'll do all twelve steps with your facilitator, at least reviewing any you've already done. The Twelve Steps are themselves an algorithm; they must be done in order.

Honesty and Responsibility

Honesty and responsibility are the foundation of this process. You are responsible for . . .

- Working only with someone you like
- Suspending your control issues for the duration (see next page)

Jen   I was enthralled when Dr. Brown told me that she would make me work and that I would be successful based upon the work that I would do on a daily basis. I was responsible for my own recovery. I would have control over the progress and success of my therapy. Our daily phone calls, as I came to understand, were not about talking to her as much as they were about me talking to myself and hearing my self-talk about my success the previous day, what stumbling blocks I had encountered, and what I did or did not do about them. She taught me that I did not have to respond to every stumbling block in my path. She even taught me that what I often was perceiving as a stumbling block was someone else's behavior, which I now know I have no control over.

- Doing the agreed-upon work in exactly the prescribed way
- Being honest with your facilitator about the daily work you are doing, what you are thinking, and what you are feeling
- Paying the agreed-upon fee, if any, for the facilitator's time
- Discontinuing the work if you find you are uncomfortable with the relationship

Control Issues

In the initial meeting with your facilitator, you should assess, together, your willingness and capacity to do the work. You must of course be committed to abstaining from chemicals throughout the process.* Further, though, the very control issues that create addiction stand in the way of doing the work of healing. To do the Fourth Step Algorithm, you must be willing and able to suspend your control issues and *just follow the directions*. The survival response of fear, control, and manipulation is strong in the face of uncovering a lifetime of accumulated emotional pain. Among the more subtle manifestations are doubt, skepticism, anxiety, and avoidance. Overthinking is a sneaky and common variation on avoidance. There is not much thinking to be done, really. Usually, you think, analyze, and then take action to get the result you want. But here, all you need to do is take action—that is, follow the directions. The result will take care of itself.

The focus on the algorithm helps to short-circuit some of these control issues. In traditional therapy, the relationship between you and the therapist is primary. Here, it is the mutual relationship to the algorithm that is primary. In short, it's easier to relinquish control to a set of directions than to a person. No one is telling you what to do, per se. Your facilitator is just that, a facilitator, not the source of the directions; he or she will be following them too. This process is a vehicle by which you will find your own answers. In addition, the simple writing of lists with which you'll begin can be manageable even if your emotional history is very painful.

Nevertheless, some people just can't suspend their control issues

---

* By "chemicals" I mean all mood-altering drugs, including antidepressants. Never stop taking prescribed drugs without consulting with the prescribing physician or psychiatrist.

Addiction Is the Symptom

> Ernie   When I began the work, I found the detailed and systematic structure and direction inherent in Dr. Brown's method to be comforting and supportive. Though I was located across the continent while we worked together, communication, by telephone, was easy. The step work, especially the fourth step inventory and fifth step sharing, helped me to discover who I am and what I want and need, as well as what I don't want and don't need. Her method directed me on a simple and gentle path that was clear and not intimidating. It kept my work simple and as emotionally neutral as possible.

long enough to complete the process. That's why a rule of the algorithm is that (barring illness or other unexpected events) if you choose not to do the work three days in a row, fail to contact your facilitator as agreed, or fail to pay as agreed, the facilitator must end the relationship. It would be unethical to do otherwise. My experience is that such a failure strongly indicates that the willingness or capacity to complete the work is not there. Further, I believe that through such lapses, some clients are unconsciously protecting themselves from trauma they are truly not prepared to face. That's why it is critical to respect this rule, and to not judge yourself or anyone else for not completing the process. The client can of course end the therapy at any time.

Daily Work

You'll work the algorithm on your own for twenty to thirty minutes a day. Some people are eager to do more—they are in a hurry to get well—but limit yourself to no more than two thirty-minute sessions. You don't want to dredge up too much history at once.

The traditional model of therapy has therapist and client meeting only once a week, sometimes twice. With this process, you'll have almost daily contact with your facilitator. This "appointment" can consist of a five- to fifteen-minute phone call or online chat, an even briefer email or text . . . whatever works best for you on a given day, whatever will strengthen you. The contact can be so brief most of the time because

> **Carolena**   Traditional therapy usually meant going in once a week to talk for an hour. Then I was on my own till next week. My first meeting with Dr. Brown offered a step-by-step program with exact instructions. I would do the work daily in the privacy of my own home. It would be about my life story, uniquely mine. I would call daily for a quick check-in, so we could deal with anything that came up immediately. Wow, I thought, this was going to be a new and very different experience. I felt like someone had my back; Dr. Brown wasn't going to let me fall flat.

the focus is on your progress with the algorithm, not on discussing old or new problems. You simply report what you accomplished since the last contact, ask any questions you might have, and if necessary discuss how to proceed. Most people need or want daily contact, especially in the beginning, although I've occasionally had a highly focused client who did well with a weekly check-in.

One reason for doing the work daily, besides healing that much faster, is to firmly establish a new habit. Remember, this process is the foundation for a spiritual house that must be maintained daily and added to throughout your life. Researchers say it takes sixty-six days to form a new habit, on average. (It can take less, but it can also take almost four times that for some people.)[20]

Write by Hand, and Not at Night

All of this work should be handwritten, in a notebook, during daylight hours. Do not write at night.

You may be tempted to take advantage of the speed and ease of your computer. Don't. First, I should note that you'd be departing from the tried-and-true directions, which would not bode well for completing the work successfully. But, second, I've always thought it somehow better to write letters than to type them, and, likewise, to write out the

---

[20] Phillippa Lally et al., "How Are Habits Formed: Modelling Habit Formation in the Real World," *European Journal of Social Psychology*, 40:6. Accessed 18 Jul. 2014, http://onlinelibrary.wiley.com/doi/10.1002/ejsp.674/abstract.

fourth-step inventory. There's nothing mechanical, nothing artificial, between heart and paper. *Twelve Steps and Twelve Traditions* notes (page 54), "Thoroughness ought to be the watchword when taking inventory. In this connection, it is wise to write out our questions and answers. It will be an aid to clear thinking and honest appraisal. It will be the first *tangible* evidence of our complete willingness to move forward."

Today, this instinct is being borne out by studies of the brain. Writing by hand and writing with a keyboard require very different brain processes. When writing by hand, the finger movements are far more complex, activating large regions of the brain involved in thinking, language, and working memory. Writing by hand actually aids cognitive development, which has implications for children's schooling. It seems to engage long-term memory too.[21] There's also evidence that reading on paper has advantages over reading from a screen. Screens, with their glare and navigational demands, are more physically and mentally tiring, which seems to make it somewhat harder to comprehend and remember what you've read. And then there's the physicality of a book (or notebook). The brain treats individual letters as physical objects, and researchers think that we may well perceive any given text in its entirety as a kind of physical landscape.[22] (I've made this book available as an e-book because the price is so accessible. But if you're reading this as an e-book and find it compelling, you might consider getting the print version—especially if you decide to undertake the work outlined here.)

Given all this, it's likely that a process such as the Fourth Step Algorithm, which seeks to deeply engage memory and learning (or unlearning, as the case may be), benefits in important ways from handwritten exercises. Think of your notebook as an externalization of your inner landscape, the better to alternately walk it and stand back from it—and then literally discard it to start anew after you complete Step Five.

There is also the fact that our keyboards are often associated with work and are attached to computers where distractions beckon. It's well

---

[21] Gwendolyn Bounds, "How Handwriting Trains the Brain," *Wall Street Journal*, 5 Oct. 2012: accessed 18 Jul. 2014, http://online.wsj.com/article/SB100014240 52748704631504575531932754922518.html.

[22] Ferris Jabr, "The Reading Brain in the Digital Age: The Science of Paper versus Screens," *Scientific American*, 11 Apr. 2013: accessed 18 Jul. 2014, http://www.scientific american.com/article/reading-paper-screens/.

> Alex   By doing the work, I gained an understanding of my deep dependence on other people, places, and situations that I had absolutely no control over. I came to understand that I was still using people to tell me I was okay. I still had the addict's mind, where the drug of choice became the approval of other people. I was so afraid they would reject or abandon me; I would let them abuse me just so they wouldn't leave. I was able to really comprehend how I gave my power away to everyone and everything.

established that getting away from our screens improves concentration.[23] Your notebook is a private, intimate space, devoted to this work and only this work.

As for writing at night: First of all, doing this work in the morning ensures that it gets done. You never know how your day is going to evolve. Second, as you make your lists, you may bring some upsetting things into consciousness, and it's best to make sure you have most of the day to clear them. It's not good to go to sleep with bad thoughts. After all, your brain doesn't stop running. You risk ruminating on these hurtful incidents at a deep level, which is exactly the opposite of what you want to achieve. Finally, most people are afraid of the dark, if in an atavistic, semiconscious way. Don't inflame your emotions by exploring your history after the sun goes down.

Self-care

Once you begin the Fourth Step Algorithm, try to give yourself some extra care. Drink more water, get enough exercise (not too much), and rest a bit more if at all possible. The process may be simple, but as I've said, it isn't always easy. As Alice Miller writes in *Thou Shalt Not Be Aware*, "The truth about childhood is stored up in our body, and although we can repress it, we can never alter it."[24] As more memories

---

[23] Ibid.

[24] Alice Miller, *Thou Shalt Not Be Aware: Society's Betrayal of the Child* (New York: Farrar, Straus and Giroux, 1998), 315.

surface, you may be surprised by the amount of anger and resentment lodged in your body. This is the emotional equivalent of toxic waste, and you need to flush it out. Many a client has likened the process to a physical detox. The first step is to put it on paper.

Also, I suggest keeping the work to yourself until it is completed. Keep your inventory in a private place, for your eyes only. Talking to people about doing it just squanders energy that could be more wisely spent on actually doing it. Besides, you may already be suspending your own skepticism; you don't want to deal with the additional doubts that might arise from a negative response, verbal or nonverbal, from someone who doesn't understand what you are doing. Some people may actively sabotage you. To the extent that you are a part of their lives, your work may mean change for them too, and even the possibility of change can cause discomfort.

Let's move on, then, to the algorithm.

Overview

Made a searching and fearless moral inventory of all relationships.

The seven phases of the Fourth Step Algorithm are summarized below. All you need to do the work is daily access to a quiet, private spot and an inexpensive notebook. If you would like to see the origins of the algorithm, page references for key portions of the Big Book and *Twelve Steps and Twelve Traditions* are collected in appendix D.

Phase 1: List your relationships A simple but thorough inventory of every person (yourself included) who has ever caused you to feel hurt in any way.

Phase 2: List incidents and feelings Any and all hurtful incidents that occurred in your relationships, and how you felt at the time. You won't dwell on them; just jot down enough to trigger the memories when you do Step Five.

Phase 3: List needs, wants, and expectations You'll look at all the incidents uncovered in phase two to explore *why* you felt hurt at the time. You'll begin to see how, since childhood, looking outside yourself to get your needs met has caused you to co-create much of your pain. You are turning the lens of emotional dependency on your life and discovering a new point of view, a new reality.

Phase 4: Review your sex life You may have covered many of your sexual relationships and encounters already, but this loaded topic needs extra attention. You'll make the same lists you did in phases one, two, and three, uncovering anything you missed with regard to sex. There's a set of questions that will ensure no stone is left unturned.

Phase 5: Review your work and finances Like sex, work and money loom large and merit some extra attention. There's a set of questions to answer in writing.

Phase 6: List principles, institutions, and fears The principles, institutions, and fears that we allow to run our lives are often hidden or unexamined. With this list, you'll bring them to awareness. You'll appraise them in Step Five, with the benefit of your facilitator's objectivity.

Phase 7: List the good All that you like and love about yourself, all that other people have told you they like and love about you, and all that you feel you've done right in your life.

As you read through the overall task, it may seem daunting. Indeed, in my counseling practice I present one phase at a time, to help my clients focus their energies on the task at hand rather than worrying about what is to come. When you actually do the work, the focus will be on one simple direction or question at a time, and you will have daily support and guidance from your facilitator. My clients invariably tell me that the actual experience is one of ease. It is possible to be both fearless and thorough in this personal inventory.

Phase 1: List Your Relationships

"Therefore, we started on a personal inventory," says the Big Book. ". . . We went back through our lives. Nothing counted but thoroughness and honesty" (pages 64–65). What does it mean to be thorough, and what does it mean to be honest? And just how thorough and honest do we have to be? "Half measures availed us nothing," we are told at the beginning of "How It Works." No half measures here; this algorithm is nothing if not thorough. The honesty is up to you.

So:

In your notebook, list every person with whom you have had a relationship in which you felt hurt in some way. I use both "relationship" and "hurt" broadly. List anyone you have come into contact with who left you feeling any kind of hurt or emotional discomfort. You may not remember the name, but the fact that you remember a bad incident or feeling suggests there might be something there worth bringing to the surface. If in kindergarten another child knocked you down, and that was the extent of your relationship, write it down: "that kid who knocked me down in kindergarten." When in doubt, list.

I liken this phase to counting nails, as if you were taking inventory of a hardware store. Each name is just a nail or a bolt. No thought other than the name that surfaces when you remember the hurt. This is absolutely not the time to ruminate. For some people, this is the biggest challenge. Don't think, just keep listing.

List your parents, siblings, other relatives, friends, spouses, lovers, bosses, classmates, teachers, priests, nuns, rabbis . . . Be sure to include authority figures of any kind. Some of these people may be deceased, but list them anyway—any hurt resulting from the relationship needs to be dealt with in the present. Don't forget "God"—the God of your childhood, the one you were given or coerced into believing in, the one that failed you.

In my experience, it is very important to look at *every single relationship* in which you have felt hurt in some way. The list can be pages long. Go back to your first recollections. For most people, memories start at about age three or four. (Scientists still aren't sure why we can't remember anything earlier, but some think that a part of the brain that contributes to recall is too undeveloped.)[25]

While working chronologically is the obvious choice, the order in which you make your list does not matter. You might not even have a choice, per se. Memories don't necessarily surface in an orderly manner. Do whatever works best for you, and don't overthink or make it complicated. It's just a list, sometimes a messy one.

There is one rule: put yourself at the top of the list. Most of us have hurt ourselves beyond measure, but often we do not see it. We have abused ourselves spiritually, emotionally, physically, and intellectually. We have allowed others to abuse us. (Abuse ranges from self-judgment to physical assault; see page 134, in appendix B.) We have failed to do the right things for ourselves. When we think about "people," I think we often forget to include ourselves. The fourth step is a way to see yourself as a person. You might never do to someone else the things you have done to yourself.

Control may raise its crafty head early on. It may appear as a nagging voice of doubt. "This is stupid," it might say as you work on your list. "Nothing is happening." "I can't remember enough. This is pointless." Or maybe, "Why am I wasting my time on this? That Dr. Brown is probably a charlatan." No offense taken for that one. Of course you have doubts. *The mind you know does not want you to escape.* Doubts may be coming from outside you as well. The collective mind is like one large dysfunctional family; it doesn't want you to escape either. But you already have one foot out the door. Just let those voices babble on in the background and keep writing.

This phase might take you a few days, or it might take you a week or more. It depends on how much time you put into the work and how many people you've had in your life.

Remember:

- You will remember what you need to remember; don't force it.
- When in doubt, list.
- Don't think, just list. You don't want to ruminate. Just keep moving.

---

[25] *Scientific American Mind* (Sept./Oct. 2012): 74.

- Overthinking is an obstruction you set up for fear of moving forward.
- Every day you pick up that pen is a good day.

— End of Phase One —

Phase 2: List Incidents and Feelings

In this phase, you will catalog what happened in your relationships with the people you listed in phase one. Turn again to your notebook. One person at a time, set up a table in the following way (see below; this is a modification of the table on page 65 of *Alcoholics Anonymous*): Write the name of the person you are going to review at the top of the page. Then make two columns. The first one is for incidents, and the second is for how each one made you feel at the time, to the best of your memory.

Now make a numbered list of every single incident you can remember in which this person hurt you, whether by what he or she said or did or did *not* say or do, followed by how you felt about it. The details of the incident are less important than the feelings. If you can't access how you felt at the time, you can probably make a good guess. But don't sit there with the pen in your hand, wondering; keep moving. If some of the people on your phase one list don't bring up anything after all, just cross them off. Note: Leave three or four blank lines after each incident (an inch or so of space); you'll need them in phase three.

When you get to yourself, remember that your inner dialogue about yourself is every bit as real as the put-downs and insults aimed at you by others. Indeed, it often constitutes an internalization of external messages.

There is nothing too small to be on this list. However, you need write only enough to trigger your memory when you go through the list with your facilitator in the fifth step. Simply note the incident with a brief descriptive phrase, jot down whatever words or phrases best describe the associated feelings, and then continue on with the incidents in numerical order. For example:

Father

Incidents	Feelings
1. Came home with a report card. All As, one B. Yelled at for B.	Sad, angry, ashamed
2. Changed his mind about the vacation we had planned.	Disappointed, angry, resentful

Try to be as matter-of-fact and objective as you can. If emotions surface, don't dwell on them, just keep moving down the list—don't think, just write. I'm going to say that again, because it's important: don't think, just write. Remember that your comfort is paramount (a priority that you will begin to carry into the rest of your life). So if you feel very agitated, put the work aside and go back to it later in the day, perhaps girded with this line from a poem a dear friend wrote to me: "Fine gifts do blossom out of dangerous, frightening places." The potential for upset is one reason for limiting the time you spend writing each day to one or two 20- to 30-minute sessions. This rule helps head off unproductive ruminating. Very quickly, you will have put in your time and can get on with your day.

When you finish with one person, choose another and repeat the process.

As you begin, don't worry about how much or how little you can dig up. People often think they won't remember much . . . and then the memories come. The more memories you lift out, the more space there is for others, long forgotten, to surface. If that's not your experience, don't worry about it. You'll remember what you need to. Even one incident can suffice to bring a dominant theme of your life to consciousness and thereby break its hold on you.

As you move through the process, you may find yourself adding to phase one's lists of relationships.

During this phase, you may (or may not) experience waves of awareness as patterns reveal themselves. Don't let them knock you down. These are previews of what is to come in Step Five. You might feel excited. You might feel nauseous. Whatever the case, put any revelations aside for later and just keep moving forward.

Remember:

- You will remember what you need to remember; don't force it. If you think of more incidents later, you can go back.
- When in doubt, list. No incident is too small.
- Don't think, just write. You are doing the work when you are moving down your list, not when you are sitting stuck.
- If you become upset, put the work aside and go back to it later in the day.

— End of Phase Two —

Phase 3: List Needs, Wants, and Expectations

Go back to your phase-two list of people and incidents. As the Big Books says (page 66), you will now consider it "from an entirely different angle." Begin at the beginning and, one at a time, look at the incidents from the angle of emotional dependency. Reread every single incident and use the space you left between them to note (preferably in red) your needs, wants, or expectations in the situation. What caused you to take the hurtful behavior, verbal or nonverbal, from the person involved?

As a child, you were vulnerable and helpless; you "took it" because you had no choice. Just write down "no choice." You may begin to uncover the repressed rage that Alice Miller talks about (see page 20). Put it aside for now and keep moving.

At some point, though, you were old enough to understand what you were doing, old enough to have made a choice. For example, all too often we will accept and internalize a put-down of no account. Think about what it means to "put down" an animal. A put-down is a killing blow to the spirit. Is it any wonder that so many of us suffer from low self-worth? Through these steps we learn to refuse such behavior, whether it comes from ourselves or others.

You may find the following questions useful. All help reveal your using mentality, the complex of fear, control, and manipulation:

· Why did I do that?
· Why did I put up with the situation or behavior?
· What did I want from that situation?
· What did I want from the other person involved?
· Why was I using that person or situation to get what I wanted?
· Was I dishonest in that relationship?
· Was I self-seeking?
· Was I frightened?
· Was I selfish?
· Was I afraid I could not get what I wanted by myself?

You will probably find that fear is involved in almost every incident. Keep listing it anyway.

When you get to your relationship with yourself, many of these questions will not apply. What did you want or expect from yourself? Don't spend too much time analyzing. The most obvious and relevant answer may be just plain fear.

For example:

Father

Incidents	Feelings
1. Came home with a report card. All As, one B. Yelled at for B.	Sad, angry, ashamed

Expected and wanted him to be proud, wanted attention for my good job.

2. Changed his mind about the vacation we had planned.	Disappointed, angry, resentful

Expected him to do what he said. Anticipation turned to disappointment and to anger.

It's helpful to be on the lookout for any time you said yes when you wanted to say no, or no when you wanted to say yes. Ask yourself what you wanted so much that you lied to yourself and others. Did you take abuse from people because they had something you thought you needed to live or just be happy?

Through the self-appraisal of this phase, you will begin to recognize your responsibility for co-creating your experiences, including relationships based on a using mentality. This is where your intellectual understanding of everything you've read here about your childhood conditioning becomes emotional—and transformational. In incident after incident, you see yourself acting out the belief that the only way you could get what you needed was to do what you were told, or to figure out what those in authority wanted you to do, or to rarely, if ever, say no to a request. You become acutely aware that you were and still are still operating, robotlike, in this fear-based control/manipulation survival mode. Seeing it in action ad nauseam, incident after incident, page after page, is quite powerful.

The so-called faults referred to in the Big Book often turn out to be no more than your quite faultless ignorance of behavioral patterns stemming from the original parent-child dynamic.

Remember:

- You will remember what you need to remember; don't force it. If you think of more incidents later, you can go back.
- Don't try to figure it out. No matter how confusing it all looks or feels right now, rest assured things will clear in Step Five.

– End of Phase Three –

Addiction Is the Symptom

Phase 4: Review Your Sex Life

Sex looms large in our culture, and there's much confusing of sex and love, so, as the Big Book recognizes, our sexual relationships merit special attention.

As you did in phase one for all relationships, list everyone with whom you've had a sexual relationship or encounter. No doubt many or even all of these people were on your initial list. That doesn't matter. You're going to put a magnifying glass to the sexual aspect of those relationships, so list them all again. Your own name should be on the list.

Once you have the list, start with the first name and make the same two-column table you did in phase two. Thinking of the sexual aspect of the relationship, list every incident you can remember in which the person hurt you, whether by what was said or done or what was *not* said or done, followed by how you felt about it at the time. The inventory of incidents should include all the times you wanted to do something and did not because of the sexual relationship. As in phase two, leave some space under each incident.

Now go back and, as you did in phase three for all relationships, look at each incident from the point of view of emotional dependency and make notes (preferably in red) in the space you left. Again, this means beginning from the age at which you could have understood whether you were trading sexual favors for something you wanted.

The following questions paraphrased from the *Twelve and Twelve* (pages 50–52) may be helpful. Remember, this isn't about beating yourself up. It's about awareness. It's about not glossing over your emotional dependency and how it may have hurt both you and others.

1. Did my pursuit of sex hurt others? Who? How?
2. Did I hurt my marriage and/or my children?
3. Did I hurt myself?
4. Did I risk my standing with friends, neighbors, or colleagues?
5. Did I feel guilty?
6. Did I absolve myself by maintaining that I was not the pursuer?
7. How did I react to sexual frustration?
8. Did I take frustration out on others?

9. If things weren't good at home, did I use that to excuse promiscuity?
10. What sexual situations made me anxious, bitter, frustrated, or depressed?
11. Looking at each situation, can I see emotional dependency at play?
12. If these problems really were caused by the behavior of others, why did I accept the behavior?

For example:

John

Incidents	Feelings
1. He refused sex.	Angry, rejected, if he loved me he would want to.

Confused sex with love. Needed him to prove he loved me with sex. Felt rejected because I didn't love myself enough.

Incidents	Feelings
2. I pretended to enjoy it when I didn't.	Anger at myself, inability to say no, afraid to say no.

Afraid he would leave me. Nowhere to go, afraid I couldn't make it on my own, honesty didn't feel like an option.

Every time you have said yes when you wanted to say no and no when you wanted to say yes, you have reinforced the numbing of your emotional being and lost a little bit of who you really are. You used your body to get what you thought you wanted or to not lose what you thought you had. Consider the effects on your life, and the high cost to you.

As for your future sex life, I like what the Big Book has to say (pages 69–70): "We remembered always that our sex-powers were God-given and therefore good, neither to be used lightly or selfishly nor to be despised and loathed. Whatever our ideal turns out to be, we must be willing to grow toward it."

Remember:

· When in doubt, list. No incident is too small.
· Don't beat yourself up. This is about awareness.
· If you become upset, put the work aside and go back to it later in the day.

— End of Phase Four —

Phase 5: Review Your Work and Finances

Like sex, work and money loom large and merit some extra attention. Where applicable, answer in writing the following questions paraphrased from the *Twelve and Twelve* (pages 51–52):

1. Have my addiction of choice and other addictive behaviors contributed to financial problems?
2. Have I let fear and doubt about my performance at work destroy my confidence?
3. If I ever felt inadequate, did I try to cover it up by lying or avoiding responsibility?
4. Or did I exaggerate my abilities, acting like a bigshot?
5. Have I had such unprincipled ambition that I undermined others?
6. Have I been extravagant with money?
7. Have I recklessly borrowed money, with no thought to repaying it?
8. Have I been cheap, failing to support my family as I should?
9. Have I cut corners financially?
10. What about "quick money," the stock market, or gambling?
11. To what extent has my emotional dependency created issues with work and money?
12. If these problems really have been caused by the behavior of others, why have I accepted the behavior?
13. If I can't change my work or financial circumstances at this time, am I willing to do something to shape my life to conditions as they are?

Remember:

· This isn't about beating yourself up. It's about awareness.

— End of Phase Five —

Phase 6: List Principles, Institutions, and Fears

The principles and institutions we live by are often a collection of other people's ideas and beliefs, most of which we did not actively choose to make our own. They may be built on nothing more than expectations. They often represent ideals or magical thinking—fairy tales for adults. Yet they may be so deeply held, you have never seen them as anything but "reality." Fears too are often hidden and unexamined. With these lists, you will bring these ideas and beliefs to the surface.

Principles In your notebook, make a list of principles that you learned in childhood and beyond. Principles are rules, sayings, or clichés that, while supposedly true, may be false and damaging to your well-being. They are often handed down from generation to generation. One that always comes to mind for me is "Children should be seen and not heard." How about "Don't rock the boat"? "A woman needs a man." Even "Honor thy father and thy mother."

Institutions Now list any institutions that have angered you or been hurtful to your well-being. An institution can be a specific organization—a church, a government. It can be an industry. The diet industry has certainly done its share of damage. An institution is also an idea organized around a collective belief about how something or someone should be controlled. Some of the more obvious are the institutions of religion, family, marriage, and heterosexuality.

Fears "This short word [*fear*] somehow touches about every aspect of our lives," reads the Big Book (pages 67–68). "It was an evil and corroding thread; the fabric of our existence was shot through with it." Indeed. List everyone and everything you are afraid of, whether you feel emotional about it or not. This is meant to capture the more abstract fears not associated with particular experiences. Fear of death often tops the list. As you write, you may find out that you have more fears tucked away than you realized.

In the fifth step, you'll appraise these lists with the help of your facilitator and begin to consider what's real and what's not. Which principles and institutions are real and true and life giving? Which should you discard? Which fears are real, and how they can be dealt with in a rational and positive way? Remember, we see what we believe. The world and your life in it may look very different once you have decided for yourself what to believe.

Remember:

- Until you are conscious of your unexamined and hidden beliefs, they are not truly yours—you cannot freely choose them.

— End of Phase Six —

Addiction Is the Symptom

Phase 7: List the Good

Finally, it is time to list all that you like and love about yourself, all that other people have told you that they like and love about you (even if you don't believe it), and all that you feel you have done right in your life, all the loving acts. This gives you a look at your true nature, at the character and integrity that's been obscured by layer upon layer of damaging social conditioning. Imagine: everything you always wanted to believe about yourself . . . all true.

When you complete the fifth step, this is the only list you will be left with. I encourage you to keep adding to it.

Remember:

· There is nothing wrong with you. What's wrong is the garbage piled on top of you—all of which you are going to throw off in Step Five.

— End of Phase Seven —

> Paul As soon as I decided that my fourth step was done and that I hadn't held anything back, I set up a time to do my fifth step. It took some hours to finish, and I told Dr. Brown everything and was totally honest. The last two-thirds of page 75 of the Big Book explain what happened to me. At that point, I really knew why I was and who I was. Old, longstanding fears dropped away. I began to feel real self-worth, and I began to like myself. Day-to-day problems like finances, power, sex relations, and even the fact that I'm HIV positive moved aside. I'm now able to walk through life without these things standing before me as if they were roadblocks.

Step Five

Admitted to God, to ourselves, and to another human being the exact nature of our relationships.

Your lists complete, you can move on to Step Five, which is done through an in-person meeting. While the fourth step is a simple, just-the-facts inventory, the fifth is an in-depth exploration. As the close companion to Step Four, it should be done as soon as possible, while all the work you put into bringing your emotional landscape to the surface is still fresh. As the Big Book says (page 75), "When we decide who is to hear our story, we waste no time. We have a written inventory and we are prepared for a long talk."

This meeting is an intensive one. On average, it takes one to three consecutive eight-hour days, with breaks, depending on the amount of fourth-step work that needs to be covered. Many people prefer the all-at-once flow of full days, but for some, shorter sessions spread over more (but still consecutive) days works better emotionally or logistically. Either way, the time involved makes a long-distance meeting unworkable, and besides, the physical presence of another is a critical part of Step Five.

The Power of a Witness

During this time, you'll relate each incident to your facilitator. This is where the emotion will come out, if it needs to. Just expressing something out loud, never mind sharing it with another, typically stirs much more feeling than thinking it or writing it down. On the other hand, some people find that, through Step Four, their perspective has already begun to shift in such a way as to take the edge off their most painful experiences.

Your facilitator serves as both witness and interpreter. As witness, he or she will validate the reality of your emotional history. As interpreter, he or she will help you to bring to consciousness the damaging patterns that have defined your life, and to see more clearly how and why you co-created so many of your hurtful experiences.

The Big Book recognizes the need for a witness. As it says on page 72, "We think we have done well enough in admitting these things to ourselves. There is doubt about that. In actual practice, we usually find a solitary self-appraisal insufficient." But it was through the work of Alice Miller that I came to truly understand its importance to the healing process. The theme throughout her work is that violence occurs because, as children, we have no witness to the violence done to us. In *For Your Own Good,* Miller refers to the "knowing or enlightened witness": someone who recognizes childhood trauma or neglect for what it is and can offer the emotional support a child needs to express his or her true feelings. Your facilitator serves the same role in relation to a whole lifetime of pain. Your Step Five work with him or her may constitute the first time you have had such a witness. It's a powerful thing. In addition, allowing another person to bear witness to your deepest, darkest secrets disposes of the fear that someone might learn about them. The

Joan   Dr. Brown guided me through her program over a six-month period, with the majority of our work together done over the telephone. Once I had completed all the writing related to the fourth step, I met with Dr. Brown for a full day, in person, and did my fifth, sixth, and seventh steps. I was finally able to let go of all the guilt, shame, and anger that had accumulated during my thirty-three years of life.

amazing result is that you no longer care what others think. This is called freedom.

In my step method, the interpretive role is also important. As you relate the emotional history collected in your notebook, incident by incident, your facilitator will help you reinterpret it via the lens of emotional dependency. You'll see that most of the time, it takes two to play the game of control and manipulation, but just one—you—to end or prevent it. With this growing awareness of co-creation comes the capacity to take personal responsibility for many of your hurtful experiences—and for refusing to engage any longer in the addictive behaviors that caused them. In other words, you understand, perhaps for the first time, that you have the power of choice. You always did. In this way, the process exposes the *un*reality of your life thus far (with its very real pain), a daymare generated by a belief system you didn't know you had. You can stop living the lies. A new reality is now yours for the choosing.

The combination of validation, awareness, and empowerment is a potent one. Finally, the accumulation of painful memories and resentment is released, spiritually, emotionally, and physically. Finally, the power we all have to shape our reality becomes, itself, real. The creative energy that rushes in can be something to behold. People actually *look* different. I've been privileged to watch and feel it happen again and again in the clients sitting across from me.

Face Your Fears

By the time you turn to the list of fears you made in Step Four, some of them may have disappeared or at least diminished. With your facilitator, you'll take a look at what's left and discuss how you might conquer or otherwise deal with them.

Trusting the God of your understanding is certainly a start. As the Big Book says (page 68), "Self-reliance was good as far as it went, but it didn't go far enough. . . . Perhaps there is a better way—we think so. For we are now on a different basis; the basis of trusting and relying upon God. We trust infinite God rather than our finite selves. . . . At once, we commence to outgrow fear."

So many of the things we tend to fear—all the bad things that can happen in life—are exceptions to the rule. Remember the phenomenon of confirmation bias, from chapter 5 (Step Two, page 44)? When you focus on these exceptions, they become all you see, and fear dominates your life. By now, you will understand the extent to which you have chosen your reality and can now choose a different one.

A mundane but, metaphorically speaking, life-threatening fear is that of making mistakes. You can become virtually paralyzed by it. "Decisions" too often consist of doing nothing. This stems in part from not knowing yourself well enough to know what you want, and in part from trying to divine the future. Once you complete this step process and a) know who you are, b) understand that you can't control the future, and c) grasp that you have the power of self-control—the power of choice—you will very likely find decisions easier. You will act based on what you want in the present, knowing that if you don't like the result, you will simply make a new choice.

Lessons Learned

Your experience of Steps Four and Five will be your own, and some of what you take from the process will be unique. But here, in the briefest of terms, are the lessons common to everyone to some degree. Most are elaborated in previous chapters. Some or all may seem obvious or even trite. However—and you can only trust me and my clients on this— Steps Four and Five give these lessons deep, experiential, life-changing meaning.

Self-control is the only control. I tell every client, "Mind your own business." That includes not spending time and energy worrying about what others are thinking or doing.

Believing is seeing. Oftentimes, the "problem" is really in your thoughts about a person or situation. Again, mind your own business.

Practice honesty. We are dishonest in direct ratio to our emotional dependency. Say yes when you mean yes, no when you mean no.

Live your truth. In other words, stop living the lies. What you have known as "reality" was just someone else's idea of it.

Stop living in fear. Fear is future-tense; life is lived in the present.

Abstain from expectations. Give to yourself what you expect from others, in the first place, love. And love freely: love expects nothing in return.

The choice is yours. Now that you truly understand that you have a choice, you can exercise it.

Pause

I strongly urge you to take some time alone after completing Step Five, a day or two not only to rest but also to get your bearings. Schedule it as part of the process. You've just entered into a new relationship with yourself and your world. Give yourself a little space to take it in. It will be the first of many new acts of critical self-care.

Out with the Old

Upon completion of this step, you will destroy your notebook, with the exception of the list of good qualities and actions you made in Step Four's phase seven. Most people like to burn it.

This destruction of your notebook, whether by fire or other means, may sound like a hackneyed ritual, but clients tell me it is surprisingly satisfying. You are done with that whole sad history, a lifetime of fear and hurt and anger. "It is so final, you can never get it back," says my client Carolena. "If it ever comes to mind, which it very rarely does, I always say to myself, 'Been there, burned that.'"

Now, from moment to moment, you will bear witness only to the good you see in yourself. In so doing, you will create a very different life, one in which beauty, not pain, is your reality. The Big Book expresses it well (page 75):

> Once we have taken this step, withholding nothing, we are delighted. We can look the world in the eye. We can be alone at perfect peace and ease. Our fears fall from us. We begin to feel the nearness of our Creator. We may have had certain spiritual beliefs, but now we begin to have a spiritual experience. The feeling that the [addiction] has disappeared will often come strongly. We feel we are on the Broad Highway, walking hand in hand with the Spirit of the Universe.

— End of Step Five —

When you are rested, you will continue the process with Steps Six through Twelve, turning back to page 56.

Chapter 7

Welcome Home

The privilege of a lifetime is being who you are.
—Joseph Campbell
Reflections on the Art of Living

As is obvious by now if you are familiar with the Twelve Steps, there is a considerable difference between my step method and what you find in *Alcoholics Anonymous, Twelve Steps and Twelve Traditions,* and fourth-step guides, and in the way the steps are practiced in twelve-step groups in general. But the biggest difference is the result. The Promises of the Big Book really do come true, and then some.

While the execution of the Fourth Step Algorithm is transparent, its outcome is highly experiential—it's hard to understand why it works unless you've done it, and hard to explain once you have. Any spiritual process that effects healing is somewhat mysterious. Consider Dr. Bernie Siegel's work with cancer patients and self-induced healing. Siegel has, since the 1970s, written extensively about the mind-body-spirit connection, including the role of consciousness and childhood experiences in disease. ("Parenting is the number one public health issue," he said in a 2008 interview.[26]) He has explained "remarkable recoveries" this way:

> The essence of the story behind remarkable recoveries can be symbol-
> ized by the image of a rainbow colored butterfly. It is the symbol of
> transformation and every color symbolizes an emotion; when your
> life is in order you are transformed and heal. It is about being born

---

[26] Carol Bedrosian, "The Art of Self-induced Healing" (31 Aug. 2008): accessed 18 Jul. 2014, http://www.spiritofchange.org/alternative-medicine/the-art-of-self-induced-healing.

again; religions and myths show us the benefit of that act. Picking a new name for yourself and changing who you are by giving up the untrue self imposed upon us by others is life saving.[27]

"Giving up the untrue self": yes. One client of mine felt so transformed, so rid of the untrue self, that she did literally "pick a new name," one that she felt fit her newfound identity. As I have described, through the Fourth Step Algorithm your individual identity is revealed—the one that got lost under all the conditioning imposed on you in childhood. Only when you know who you really are can you know what you really want—and seize the power to achieve it.

To rediscover your true self, to come home, is a revelation. One of my clients, after finishing his step work with me, said, "All my life I've been looking for the perfect person to love . . . the one who would love me the way I need to be loved. Now I know that person is me." Love for oneself is indeed life saving.

If there is a more formal construct through which to understand my step process, it's what psychologists call catharsis: the elimination of a complex—here, the complex of fear, control, and manipulation—by bringing it to consciousness and giving it expression. I think of it as "psyche surgery," akin to a physical surgery that removes every last bit of a malignant tumor. Incident after incident, page after page, the Fourth Step Algorithm roots out a lifetime of repressed feelings, memories, resentments, and unconscious beliefs. The fifth step, through sharing them with a witness, expresses and purges them. The eighth and ninth steps offer further cleansing. The leap in consciousness, the spiritual renewal, is quantum because the process is so thorough.

Free of a false self, you know who you are, irrespective of the criticism or praise of others. With that comes an understanding of what you really want. Free of the burden of the past, you can begin again, from the present. Finally, you can move forward to fulfill your potential.

I've long admired the Austrian psychiatrist Viktor Frankl, founder of logotherapy/existential analysis, a meaning-centered approach to psychotherapy. A Holocaust survivor, he is familiar to many as the au-

---

[27] Dr. Bernie Siegel, "Self Induced Healing and Remarkable Recoveries" (19 May 2011): accessed 18 Jul. 2014, http://berniesiegelmd.com/2011/05/self-induced-healing-and-remarkable-recoveries/.

Carolena   My work with Dr. Brown exceeded any expectation I had at the beginning. I had always felt small and vulnerable, and fear ruled my life. Everything I did or did not do was based in fear and self-doubt. The courage I've gained has given me true freedom to do what I want to do, to do what brings me joy. What others think, say, or do has no dominion over my decisions or actions. I no longer feel lost.

My marriage has changed profoundly. The tension between us is gone, and the fun and laughter have returned. My husband is no longer on edge when I am around. I know I am responsible for myself and my own happiness in this marriage.

Dr. Brown often reminded me, "You can only give what you have. If you are looking outside yourself to get your needs met, you are not giving anything, you're bargaining." I now have a self to bring to any situation I encounter, and I now know that I have a lot to give. My life is filled with profound gratitude and love for myself and others.

thor of *Man's Search for Meaning*. Dr. Frankl loved heights. He was a mountain climber and, starting late in his life, a pilot. According to biographer Anna S. Redsand, he liked to include experiences from both climbing and flying in his lectures. In one such lecture, she writes, he explained how, in a crosswind, a pilot must aim the plane not at his goal but beyond it. "He said that it was like this with human beings. If we expect something higher of ourselves, we will reach what we are actually capable of. If we aim only for what we are capable of, we are likely to achieve beneath our abilities."[28] He sometimes referred to logotherapy as "height psychology," which would have people focus on the best and highest in themselves, in contrast to depth psychology, which probes the unconscious mind for what's wrong.

My step method includes both depth and height, on the premise that it is only when you do the emotional work of digging deep to un-

---

[28] Anna S. Redsand, *Viktor Frankl: A Life Worth Living* (New York: Clarion Books, 2006), 118–119.

earth the jewel of the self — "to bring forth what you are, and what you might be," as Joseph Campbell wrote—that you can reach the heights of your full potential. The Fourth Step Algorithm is the cornerstone of that work.

Key Concepts

Healing Within the context of addictive behavior, healing is a process that produces a qualitative change in the consciousness of the addicted person. This change restores choice.

Psychology The root of the word, *psyche,* means "soul." The process outlined in this book is a form of soul, or spiritual, therapy.

Chapter 8

Your Healing Is Up to You

The knight in shining armor, the person who is going to rescue me from my life, is me. I am the one I was always looking for.
—Chris, former client

Now you know that you have a choice between addiction/relapse and healing. The question is, are you willing to do the work of healing? There will be obstacles before you even begin the step process, both within and without. You will have to push past your own fears, and you will have to find a qualified facilitator who is willing and able to give you precisely the help you need. But in so doing, you will get your first small taste of freedom from the emotional dependency that drives addiction. Healthy self-reliance starts here.

The Obstacles Within

Heretofore, addiction has been the core of your life; now healing must be the center around which everything revolves. In this way, your life will become a reflection of healing rather than of addictive behavior. But as noted in previous chapters, most people are not willing to do the work of healing. Resistance to doing the Twelve Steps even in their traditional form, never mind in the more intensive form outlined in this book, is the norm. Why?

Some people fear failure. They think they won't be able to do the work adequately and won't achieve the promised results. Some fear that they will not have the strength to face the accumulated emotional trauma that will be uncovered in the fourth step. Others are just plain unwilling to put in the time.

If you fear failure, that's understandable. Until now, doing the

Twelve Steps has been an often confusing trial-and-error process with little, if any, assurance of success—relapse being the ultimate result for the majority. Perhaps you've relapsed many times. Perhaps you've already spent thousands of dollars on both traditional and alternative therapies that seemed to offer hope but finally left you demoralized. Another disappointment would be too much to bear. Now, though, you have a set of simple, precise, time-tested directions that promise a much higher likelihood of success. As I've said, people with all kinds of problems—drug addiction, sex addiction, binge eating—have found healing by faithfully completing the modified step process outlined in this book. Those who have been abstinent for years have found new levels of emotional freedom and self-determination. And further, those who simply wanted answers to the question "Who am I?" or "Is this all there is?" have found their answers. All they did was follow the directions.

If facing your emotional history frightens you, that's understandable too. It can be scary to look back at where you've been. But you need to suspend your self-protective control issues only long enough to follow the directions for twenty minutes each day. And you won't be alone: you'll have daily support from your facilitator. If it really is too much for you, you will simply stop.

As for being unwilling to put in the time . . . I can only assume that you haven't yet hurt enough to make healing a priority. Those who are in the most pain have, in this respect, an advantage. They are desperate to heal, and they take to the work with an acute understanding that their very lives depend on it. But as you now know, we're all addicted to one degree or another. We all have control issues that can deform our lives. Just ask yourself whether you think someone in your life needs to change, to stop or start doing something. That thinking is usually the precursor to some kind of action (or inaction) meant to change the person to suit your needs. That's the complex of fear, control, and manipulation at work. When your control efforts are thwarted, resentment is sure to follow, with its accompanying pain . . . and so on. As you accumulate resentments, your life can only darken.

Wherever you live on the addiction spectrum, the extent to which you heal yourself of emotional dependency is the extent to which you will become powerful in your own right, largely free of fear, and able to reach your full potential as a human being.

The Obstacles Without

Over the years, I've encountered a disheartening resistance in the treatment and mental health communities to the very notion of healing addiction. Unfortunately, that creates an external obstacle for you. I hope I'm wrong, but you may find that few of the people you would typically turn to for help will be willing facilitators of the healing process outlined here.

When I finished my graduate program in 1993 and then in 1995 saw part of my dissertation published in *Alcoholism Treatment Quarterly*, I expected to find a treatment center that would see my work as an enhancement to its program. The Twelve Steps were at the core of most treatment programs, after all. Allied with a treatment center, I would be able to create a healing institute, train other psychotherapists, work with clients, and generate empirical studies of results. Instead, from coast to coast, I found a total lack of interest in even the idea of healing addictive behavior.

After countless meetings with directors of treatment centers, heads of residential and outreach programs, and administrators of federal and state funding for treatment programs, I finally understood the resistance. What I heard from all of these people could be summed up in one response: "What you say makes perfect sense, but insurance pays for relapse." Just as the real money is to be made in war, not peace, the real money is to be made in unending addiction—in the cycle of "recovery" and relapse—not healing. Given the proliferation of single-addiction step programs, it also seemed clear to me that relapse was on the rise, and that the more lucrative the system became, the harder it would be to change it. Also around that time, as over two-thirds of US residential treatment centers closed their doors because of cutbacks imposed by the insurance industry, the whole ineffectual, self-interested production was being repackaged for outpatient programs.

I had no more luck out in the mental health community. With at least seven out of ten AA participants falling into relapse with alcohol (and even more with substitute addictions), would no one welcome a twelve-step process that had proved effective? One that worked not only for people with chemical and process addictions, but also for anyone who had control issues? Again, the bottom line, in my experience, was that too many of those providing addiction treatment believed that healing would mean losing money.

Institutions may be particularly resistant to change, but individuals can put up a good fight as well. For professional therapists, weekly, talk-heavy visits that can carry on indefinitely are standard. My intensive, work-focused, and relatively brief process is quite different. Many of the professionals with whom I've spoken over the years don't want to take the risk of trying something new—or just can't be bothered to—when their work is lucrative just as it is.

I once phoned a New York psychoanalyst to ask that he read an early, never-published version of this book or at least allow me to tell him about my research. He kindly listened to a brief account of my results and then said, "What do you want from me?" When I told him I would appreciate his reading my manuscript because I felt I needed a clinician's reaction, he said it was out of the question. "I have a conference to attend . . . " I could have accepted that response as perfectly reasonable, as I had many similar responses, were it not for an earlier comment he'd made: "It sounds as though it would work for a patient of mine." He was not interested enough in the well-being of that patient to ask me more about the process or to refer the patient to me.

A more insidious obstacle is the culture of talking. It was once the norm to talk about deeply personal matters hardly at all. Now the culture has shifted to the extreme opposite, in which people think nothing of spending years in talk therapy. Too often, people talk endlessly about their problems rather than doing something about them, whether in their daily lives, formal therapy, or a step group.

When I was a few years sober, I was at an AA meeting and another member said to me, "Why don't you shut up and stop talking about your problems and work the program?" And then there was the time that a member said to me, "Guess where you're going to be ten years from now." I smiled and said, "I have no idea." She responded, "You'll be right where you are today, only ten years older." At that moment, I could not imagine being where I was, in my head, for ten more days, let alone ten more years.

"Shut up and work the program" is not an admonition that would be heard in twelve-step meetings today. But early in the program and into the 1970s, there would usually be some "old-timers" sitting at the back of the room, and if anyone at the podium were to go on about something that had little or nothing to do with the program, one of them might shout, "Hey! Why don't you take the cotton out of your ears, put it in your mouth, sit down, listen, and learn something!" People would laugh, and the speaker would blush and sit down. Everyone knew it was well-meant. The old-timers knew too well that the task at hand was a matter of life and death.

It was comments such as these that motivated me to do what I had to do: work the program, meaning work the steps. As long as I could get someone to listen to and sympathize with my problems, I was on a downward spiral. It was only when I did shut up and start working the program that my life began to change. Even in their traditional, symptom-focused form, the steps help.

To be clear, I am not completely dismissing "talk therapy." As I've noted, talk has its place. It relieves pressure and can in fact be lifesaving. But how many therapists have you tried? Over how many years? If you've ever worked with a good one, you've probably experienced the high of an "aha" moment or two—only to be disappointed when the revelation didn't change anything. Talking might shed light on problems, but it doesn't *solve* them. And at its worst, talk therapy forces you to repeatedly relive traumatic experiences, magnifying them instead of defusing them.

For all these reasons, there's a dearth of professionals who have experience with my step method. I hope this book will begin to correct that situation. Meanwhile, to do the work itself, you may have to first do the work of finding a therapist or counselor who is as willing as you are to step up to the task.

Finding a Facilitator

From time to time I am asked, "Can I do the work by myself?" Or, "Can't I do this with my sponsor?" My response is that you and only you can do the work, but, as I've touched on, I believe professional support is important to the successful completion of this process, especially of the Fourth Step Algorithm and its companion, Step Five.

If you are not familiar with step programs, let me fill you in on sponsorship. New members are admonished to get a sponsor as quickly as possible and to rely on him or her when the going gets tough. The assumption is that even a member who has been on the program for a short time has something to offer someone who just walked through the door. So your sponsor can be anyone who has been on the program longer than you have. (In fact, it's suggested that you in turn sponsor others as soon as possible.) The only caveat is to choose a winner, someone who appears to be working the program successfully.

Members of AA and other twelve-step programs generally find sponsorship rewarding. For the sponsors, it's a gratifying opportunity to share their experience, strength, and hope. For the sponsees, it means a willing listener, a social contact, and usually a friend who will be there to help, whatever the need. In the beginning, sponsorship also helps you achieve and maintain abstinence. Research has indicated that AA members who reach out frequently and consistently to their sponsors (and other fellow members) fare better than those who do not.[29]

Consequently, it may feel natural to turn to a sponsor for help with my step method; you might even feel pressured to do so. But considering the very high likelihood that any given sponsor's control issues are at the high end of the spectrum, even after years of abstinence from a primary addiction, I can't be confident that the instructions in this book would be understood and executed as they should be. I am much more comfortable recommending a professional.

What about a sponsor who has completed my step process? While I believe that anyone (in or outside the program) who has personally completed the process is potentially qualified to facilitate it, in the absence of a certification program that can affirm their preparedness, again, I am more comfortable recommending a professional.

First, by virtue of their training and experience, professionals are presumably more likely than nonprofessionals to grasp the foundation of my work and its psychological components. This can only be an aid to your success.

Second, while the Fourth Step Algorithm is somewhat mechanical, Step Five requires solid interpretive skills on the part of the facilitator. A talented, experienced professional will bring invaluable insight and intuition to this step.

---

[29] Mary Sheeren, "Relationship Between Relapse and Involvement in Alcoholics Anonymous," *Journal of Studies on Alcohol,* vol. 49, no. 1 (1988): 104–106.

Third, you may recall the research, cited earlier, that reported of the fourth step, "In attempting such a self-evaluation outside of a therapeutic relationship, these alcoholics had become anxious and acted out by drinking again."[30] While that finding concerns the traditional approach to Step Four, whose primary difficulties I believe I have addressed with the Fourth Step Algorithm, caution is still in order. Digging into your emotional history can be scary. Most people underestimate the amount of pain and anger they've accumulated. My experience is that anyone who sticks with the process is in fact ready to face this pain and anger, difficult though it may be. The Fourth Step Algorithm is designed to protect those who are not. But a professional will presumably be equipped to get you through anything that does comes up in both the fourth and fifth steps, or to quickly refer you to someone who can.

Finally, this process requires of the facilitator a certain rigor and emotional stamina, both of which come with the territory of professional practice.

The ideal facilitator would of course be a professional therapist or counselor who has personally completed the work—thereby addressing his or her own emotional dependency—and also facilitated the work before. Given that only with this book has my step method finally gone public, such people will be few and far between for a while. How, then, do you find a qualified facilitator with whom to do this work? Here are some guidelines for your search:

· Your facilitator should be someone who has read and understood this book, as well the companion facilitation guidelines (available for free download at my website).
· He or she must be willing to follow the directions as precisely as you must be. I may sound like a broken record on this point, but experience tells me I can't say it enough. There could be a natural tendency to slip into talk therapy or to complicate the directions. Either could result in the very mode of symptom focus and trial and error that, I believe, too often makes the traditional steps a recipe for relapse.

---

[30] Hendrik Lindt, "The Rescue Fantasy in Group Treatment of Alcoholics," *Journal of Group Psychotherapy,* vol. 9 (Jan. 1959): 43–52.

- The key is a willingness to try something new. Such willing therapists exist. They are as frustrated as you are by the failures of talk therapy. They too are searching for what works. And they are more concerned with helping than with filling their schedules. If you are very lucky, you are already working with such a therapist.
- The therapist must be willing to suspend any belief in the widely unquestioned premise that addictions are chronic. That is, he or she must believe that healing is a possibility.
- As this process is essentially a spiritual solution, albeit one with powerful psychological components, the therapist should have spiritual leanings and/or spiritual openness.
- Familiarity with addiction issues and the traditional Twelve Steps may be useful but is not necessary.

Be prepared to interview several people. Most professionals will talk at least briefly on the phone about their experience and approach. You can use such a conversation to gauge their willingness to add something new to their therapeutic repertoire. You might direct them to this book or to my website to learn more. It should be possible to make an exploratory appointment with the most promising candidate. Before agreeing to a consultation, the therapist or counselor might want some time to read the materials and think about the logistics of this new mode of therapy.

The right professional is probably the one who, after due consideration, is as excited as you are to begin.

Revolution

The idea that addictive behavior can be healed is new. This idea challenges the conventional wisdom. It challenges a very lucrative, but unsuccessful, model of treatment. The system, like most, is slow to change. Meanwhile, your best self remains unknown to you. You yearn for release from the addictive behaviors that are crippling your one and only life. You have waited long enough. And only you can end that wait.

Start a revolution within by having just a little faith in yourself and your God-given capacity to heal. Start a revolution without by demanding treatment that works. Come to your own rescue. If not today, when?

Chapter 9

A Plan for Independent Living

**We cannot allow anything to come between us and our spiri-
tuality, or between us and our living process. If we do, we shall
destroy ourselves and those around us.**

—**Anne Wilson Schaef**
When Society Becomes an Addict

Imagine now that you've completed the work outlined in this book.
You are experiencing, as one of my clients put it, "an utterly altered
sense of existence."

Through these steps, the unique and independent self that was bur-
ied beneath a lifetime of conditioning has emerged. The voices of others,
which you thought were your own, have gone quiet; you have found

---

Jen   As of this writing, I've been sober for almost seventeen
months, and it's been just a little over a year since I started
working with Dr. Brown. Sometimes it seems like years, because
I am so far removed from the person I was thirteen months ago.

When we started, I perceived that the work would help to keep
me sober, which was my only goal at the time . . . to stop drinking, abstinence! But as I came out the other side after ninety days,
the work was about changing me, not just abstaining. It's not just
about not drinking and counting the days away from my last drink,
but about looking forward and knowing that I deserve a full, wonderful life of my own choosing.

This is more than not drinking. This is life changing.

---

your own voice. You are no longer emotionally dependent on others for the answers to how to live your life; you have found your own answers. You are no longer dependent on others for your deepest needs; you have learned that you can rely on yourself and the God within you. You know who you are. You know what you want. And you are empowered to achieve it. You are free.

You have also grasped that every conflict you've ever had was a rerun of a behavioral model you learned in childhood—the complex of fear, control, and manipulation. That user mentality never worked, and it never will. Through your newfound awareness and self-reliance, it is withering away. When addictive behavior does surface, you now have the awareness and the tools to quickly reject it. And so all your relationships are becoming more loving and respectful, including your relationship with yourself.

There's no way you want to go back. Yet you also know that the habit of emotional dependency is strong. How could it be otherwise, when it was woven into your psychic fabric so early and so thoroughly? As good as you feel upon completing this twelve-step process, your healing has only begun. Its expansion to every corner of your life hinges on the development of all areas of self-reliance.

You need a plan. A "business" plan. Your life is your business, and you're the only one you want running it.

Independence Defined

First, let's explore just what this newfound "independence" means, the very idea of it being quite foreign to most people with addictions.

A dictionary is a helpful guide to its full dimensions. Mine defines *independent* as, among other things, "not subject to control by others: self-governing"; "not requiring or relying on something else"; "not looking to others for one's opinions or for guidance in conduct"; "not requiring or relying on others (as for care or livelihood)." Synonym: *free*.[31]

Free in turn is defined as, among other things, "enjoying personal freedom: not subject to the control or domination of another"; "not

---

[31] *Merriam-Webster's Collegiate Dictionary,* 11th Edition (Springfield, MA, 2004), 633.

> **Alex** Because of my work with Dr. Brown, I no longer seek outside myself for fulfillment or satisfaction. I have been empowered to set into action the future I always wanted but had shelved. Deep inside, I was waiting for the right person or circumstances to come along and save me! Today I am self-reliant, and every day I put my energies into becoming more self-reliant and creating the beautiful life I want for myself. Fear doesn't prevent me from taking action.
>
> I now seek my own counsel. I don't defer my instincts or my intelligence to anyone, especially not authority figures. I trust myself implicitly. I have a sense of myself as being whole like I remember being as a child, but now it is so much greater because of my new level of consciousness.
>
> My ability to concentrate and absorb things has dramatically increased because I no longer have racing thoughts and split thinking. I can focus all my attention on the task at hand. My addictive, dependent mind has healed. As a result I have gone back to school in addition to working full time, and I'm enjoying every bit of it. The satisfaction is coming from the work I'm doing, from my own efforts, and it is so sweet! I had no experience of how marvelous I could feel about myself, when all that has changed is my own level of consciousness.
>
> Words can't convey my gratitude. I have a second chance at life.

determined by anything beyond its own nature or being: choosing or capable of choosing for itself"; "relieved from or lacking something and especially something unpleasant or burdensome"; "not subject to restriction or official control"; "not obstructed, restricted, or impeded"; "not being used or occupied"; "not hampered or restricted in its normal operation"; "frank, open"; "not united with, attached to, combined with, or mixed with something else." Synonyms: *independent, sovereign, autonomous.*[32]

My dictionary also notes that *independent* "implies a standing

---

[32] Ibid., 498.

> **Paul** The outside things came back to me very quickly. I now own a house, a boat, and a car. I meditate quietly every day for ten to fifteen minutes. Even now I continue to remember things that happened in the past. I quickly ask for help, put them in perspective, and make amends if I have to. I keep in touch with my Higher Power and my close friends in the Fellowship. My life today is many times better and more full and meaningful than I could ever have imagined six years ago.

alone," while *free* "stresses the complete absence of external rule and the full right to make all your own decisions."

Alone vs. Lonely

The implications of independence may have you feeling a mix of excitement and unease. The aspect of "standing alone" might be especially threatening, but independence will elude you until you learn how to make yourself happy when you are by yourself.

"Alone" conjures up isolation, even solitary confinement. As a child, you may have been punished with isolation. Such scoldings as "go to your room and stay by yourself until you can do as you're told" are not readily forgotten. And then there is *alone*'s association with rejection. When I was growing up, there was a popular song titled "You're Nobody 'til Somebody Loves You." What a message. The result of these deep associations is that we are too often willing to engage in any form of dependency to avoid the assumed consequences of being alone.

However, *alone* need not be synonymous with *lonely*—loneliness being a hallmark of addiction. For a healthy person, the experience of being alone is far removed from that of being lonely. Once you experience the reality of independence—of standing alone—perhaps for the first time in your life, there is very little that will induce you to again be subject to another. Dependency, after all, allows for little if any choice. Choice is the reward for the work of living an independent life. And it does take work. There will be moments of self-doubt. But the end result is a strong and well-deserved sense of pride.

Responsibility

What is the work of independence? Responsibility. Your new life of self-reliance, in contrast to the old one of other-reliance, entails a level of responsibility that few people are accustomed to. Responsibility is usually thought of as a burden, a duty, no fun at all . . . not something to seek out. But if you instead think of it as "response-ability," it takes on an entirely different connotation. It's about your willingness and *ability* to *respond* to life—to be responsible for yourself in all areas of your life—rather than depend on others to respond for you. Responsibility is what frees you from the ideas, desires, whims, and approval of others, so that you may pursue your own unadulterated version of fulfillment.

Inter-Independence

You may be asking yourself just how other people *do* figure into this new existence. I remember doing an evaluation with a woman who, after I explained the work and the outcome, said, "Oh, but if I do that I won't have any more boyfriends." I tried to explain that until she changed her consciousness, she might have any number of boyfriends—but the relationships would very likely continue to begin and end in dysfunction.

"Independent" does not mean without relationships. Of course not: interdependence is an unavoidable and potentially rich part of the human condition. But too often, interdependence is characterized by addictive behaviors. How could it be otherwise, when we as individuals are driven, to one degree or another, by emotional dependency? Before you completed the steps, healthy relationships may have eluded

Ernie   Today, I credit the quality of my life to the work I did with Dr. Brown, and especially the insight I gained through her method of taking the fourth step. My life still includes trials and difficult times, as does everyone's. But because I gained a deep understanding of the role fear plays in every relationship and decision, I have been able to return continually to the methods Dr. Brown taught me to see clearly the way to serenity.

you. Now that you are no longer dependent on others for your happiness or anything else, and you've become whole as an individual, the old inter-*de*pendence can become what I like to call inter-*in*dependence.

Inter-independent relationships are based not on needs or wants (expectations), but on genuine mutual regard. The realization that you can't be responsible to or for another person—children and the infirm excepted—eliminates the usual confusion between need and love.

What does inter-independence look like?

The fear that underlies so many relationships, whether acute or vague, evaporates. It was the fear that if you didn't fulfill others' needs or expectations, they'd abandon you. As an independent person, you no longer fear being alone. The people in your life can enhance it, but they can't take anything away from it. You are now free to say yes when you want to say yes, and no when you want to say no—a significant breakthrough in mental health—so your relationships can be more honest, which in turn enables deep trust. And conflict is rare. Most conflict arises from fear, control, and manipulation, and that complex has been broken. Because you've learned self-acceptance, you are more accepting of others' foibles, and respectfulness in all your interactions is the norm. You have no need to put others down to feel good about yourself. And when you ask others for help, as we all must from time to time, you are prepared to accept no for an answer without resentment, and you intuitively avoid people who expect "payback."

In intimate relationships, love, not sex, is the foundation. The focus is on each individual supporting the other in achieving his or her potential and in being fully expressive along the way. The same focus is brought to the construct of "family," which ceases to be possession oriented, territorial, and even warlike. Neither children nor adults are objects to be controlled. Rather, a peaceful "live and let live" attitude prevails. When you encourage and support yourself and live your life fully, you can afford to allow others to do the same.

It would be nice if all the people you know were to do the work of freeing themselves of emotional dependency, but they don't have to change in order for your relationships with them to improve. It takes two to play the game of fear, control, and manipulation, and you're no longer playing it.

> **Joan** As a result of the step work that I completed with Dr. Brown, my regular participation in AA meetings, and my complete faith in God, I am a different person. Today, my fears and insecurities are minimal. I begin each day with a prayer, turning my life and my will over to God and asking Him to show me His will throughout the day. If I am struggling during the day, I say the serenity prayer or simply "help me." Fears and insecurities are no longer running my life. I am happy with who I am and enjoying discovering my own unique personality, an identity that has always been a mystery to me. I am living in the moment, appreciating little things like a bright, sunny day, petting a purring cat, and taking a nap. I now can even appreciate the rain. I am finally enjoying being alive, one day at a time.

A Comprehensive Plan

If you underwent surgery to treat a disease caused by lifestyle, you would want to change your lifestyle so as to avoid a recurrence of the problem. It is the same here. The surgery is not the end, but the beginning. How do you ensure that you don't slip back into old habits? How do you continue your growth and deepen your healing? Right away, you need to get a basic maintenance plan in place. Second, you need to build your spiritual practice. Third, you need to gradually expand self-reliance to all areas of your life.

1. Basic Maintenance

Basic maintenance of the results of my step process entails three things: (a) refusing to feed energy into the past, (b) working the steps daily, and (c) staying current.

Refuse the past It's well established that memories degrade if we don't use them, whereas what we dwell on or rehash in conversation becomes magnified in consciousness, impossible to let go. So after the fifth step, when any unwanted part of the past returns to thought, remind yourself that you've dealt with it once and for all through this work, dismiss the

Chris Because of all my detailed work with Dr. Brown years ago, when I do a written fourth step now, I have no resentments, fears, or concerns from the past, just from the present.

The serenity prayer was my mantra for my first AA years, but since being introduced to the Twelve Steps in this way, they are now my mantra. Each day when I meditate, I go through each step to see if I'm missing something that I can do with them. During the day, I do the same. I've learned that my life journey is to find ways to be able to live happily, not so much with others, but with myself. I'm the person I try to escape from with my addictions. From my sadness, anger, fear, and recognition of the fact that, lover or no lover, friends or no friends, I am alone in this world. Before co-dependency recovery, I couldn't accept that, because I thought I didn't have the faculties to live without a man.

My success isn't measured financially, but spiritually. I was able to move to an area of the country without friends to support me there, just myself. I recently left a job that I took out of fear, because I know I deserve better. I love to help others, but I have become the most important person in my life. My entire day is not spent trying to ensure that no one is angry with me.

Through this twelve-step process I've been able to learn that the knight in shining armor, the person who is going to rescue me from my life, is me. I am who I was always looking for.

---

memory, and turn your thoughts to the present. To reengage with your history (thinking about past injuries real or imagined, talking about them, justifying your anger, etc.) is to risk defeating the purpose of all your work. The only reason to talk about these things is to help someone else. Even then, thanks to Steps Four and Five, your interpretation will be much different from before.

When you no longer feed energy into the past with your thoughts and words, it will no longer warp your experience of the present. Your present can be shaped instead by the positive, healthy choices you are able to make now that your mind is no longer cluttered, your spirit no longer bound, by a past that you did not truly choose.

Work the steps daily From time to time, you will likely find yourself slipping into old emotional habits. The steps are an effective intervention tool. Put them to use anytime you find yourself trying to control a person, place, thing, situation, or substance, starting with admitting your powerlessness over all of the above. By applying the steps continually, you can avoid addictive behavior or stop it when it surfaces. Any history that somehow escaped your initial fourth step can also be addressed as it comes up. Over time, the habit of control will wane.

Stay current Now that you've dealt with the past, you want to stay current. That is, you want to keep your consciousness clear, free of any new accumulation of pain and resentment. So every three months to a year, do Steps Four and Five again starting from the date of your last inventory. Do Steps Eight and Nine, the amends steps, too. As Step Ten says, when we are wrong we promptly admit it . . . but sometimes promptness eludes the best of us. This is the time to consider whether you have overlooked or neglected anything. You can now do Step Four on your own. Step Five's witness role can now be filled by a sponsor, spiritual advisor, therapist, or any other trusted counselor. If you are doing the steps on a daily basis, there may come a time when you rarely need a witness.

2. Spiritual Practice

I've stated many times in these pages that the Twelve Steps are the foundation of a spiritual life, one that frees us from the complex of fear, control, and manipulation—from addictive behavior. This deeply conditioned complex is pushed deeper and deeper into the background through practice. You *can* graduate from "the program," but not from its principles, the steps.

Any twelve-step program is important to the extent that you use it to support your spiritual process. Some people use the program very well—it is all they need to sustain a full spiritual life. As time goes on, you may choose to expand your spiritual life beyond the program, which may or may not mean leaving the program.

I have a friend, an AA member for thirty-five years, who meditates, attends one meeting a week, and runs through Steps One, Two, and Three in the shower every morning and Steps Four and Five as needed. The other steps have become automatic. That's just one example of a simple, effective spiritual practice. What might yours look like?

Spiritual fitness is very much like physical fitness: you don't get fit and then stop, or you'll find yourself out of shape once again. If you let anything come between you and your spiritual life, relapse in one form or another is inevitable. Through the steps you released yourself from your addictive behavior, discovering a whole new way of being. Keep practicing them, and you will maintain your freedom and grow freer still as you evolve emotionally and spiritually.

3. Expanding Self-reliance

When people think of independence, all too often only one aspect of it comes to mind: financial independence. However, independence has five important aspects: spiritual, emotional, intellectual, physical, and yes, economic. If you are to continue your progress toward an independent life, each of these must be addressed.

It is only through self-analysis that any of us can understand the degree to which we are independent. In the appendix, you'll find some questionnaires that may help you evaluate and further your progress.

Spiritual independence Spiritual independence is about choosing for yourself that which is life giving and rejecting that which is not. Are your thoughts, words, actions, reactions, and relationships spiritual? You can choose which thoughts to feed energy into and which ones to ignore. You can choose the words you use, the actions you take, the reactions you have. You can choose with whom you spend your time. All these choices and more create your experiences—your life.

Emotional independence What do you do each day to show love toward yourself? Are you still waiting for others to give to you or do for you what you need or want? How do you talk to yourself? Do you continue to allow others to speak to or act toward you in ways that are less than loving and respectful?

I always tell clients to buy what they want for themselves rather than waiting for someone else to do it. After all, only you know what you want. Aren't you tired of getting what other people think you want? Or deserve? You deserve the best. Go get it, and don't forget to thank yourself for being so smart. I had a client, a middle-aged man, who had always wanted a leather jacket but did not have enough self-worth to buy the one he wanted. After completing his step work and realizing his own value, he finally bought it. Another client bought herself a beautiful doll similar to one she was promised as a child but never did get. Another joined a choir. She'd always wanted to sing with a group, but in the early grades she was in a play, and the teacher told her to lip-synch so she wouldn't spoil the singing. She never sang again—until she completed her twelve-step work using my method. These are small but important miracles.

Intellectual independence Do you know how smart you are? Do you know that you are potentially capable of doing exceptional work in an area of your choosing? Many people are unaware of their native abilities because they compare themselves to others with different abilities, abilities they can't possibly compete with. The only valid comparisons to make are between where you were, where you are now, and where you want to go. And it is never too late to find your gifts and then use them to achieve your goals. I got my PhD at age sixty-one, thank you.

Physical independence Do you know your body? What do you do each day to care for it? Consider the food you eat, the exercise you do.

Today, there is no shortage of people telling all of us what we should eat, how we should exercise, what we should look like, how much we should weigh . . . But when we act on dogma, trends, and other external pressures, we may not be serving our unique physical needs and realities. In the end, each of us must take responsibility for discovering and meeting those unique needs—we must each become our own best authority on our own body.

Consider too how your thoughts and conversations affect your physical being. When you feed your mind, you are also feeding your body, through the mechanisms of stress and self-fulfilling prophecy. Your thoughts very much determine both your bodily health and the physical circumstances in which you find yourself—your *in*-vironment determines your environment. Fortunately, you have control over the former.

Economic independence Are you financially independent? If not, why? What can you do about it?

Economic independence is essential for healthy relationships. How can you possibly have an honest, equal relationship with someone if you are dependent on him or her to take care of you financially? If you want money from them? You can't. Too many women, especially, still fall into the trap of becoming financially dependent on partners who use money to control them. When they break free of that control, the money disappears, sometimes with dire consequences.

This is not to say that you can't, for example, be a stay-at-home mom or dad and forgo earning money for your work. You and your partner do however need to arrange your financial lives such that each of you has money to call your own.

Test: Yes and No

Is your plan working? If you want to know whether you are independent, an easy self-test is to pay attention to how often you say yes when you want to say no, or no when you want to say yes. As I touched on in chapter 5's discussion of honesty (page 52), either is a form of lying, the chief casualty of which may be you.

Independent people generally say yes when they want to say yes, and no when they want to say no. And they don't feel compelled to explain themselves when they say no. No one expects you to explain when you say yes (i.e., when you tell them what they want to hear). Why should it be different when you say no?

The compulsion or sense of obligation to explain dates back to childhood, when we were punished for saying no. "Don't you dare say no to me, I'm your mother!" (or father or some other authority figure). Children learn to say no and what it means at around age two. Little by little, though, the power of no is wrested away. It's all about who's going to be boss. The winners are those with the power, those who are bigger and louder and more ferocious. In this way we learn to control or be controlled.

Think about the last time you said yes when you wanted to say no and ask yourself why you did it. You may tell yourself that you did not want to offend or hurt the person involved. It's true that the most polite no can be taken as a rejection. In that case, you are not responsible for "making" the person feel anything; you need not apologize for your honesty. An appropriate response is, "I hope you feel better soon." However, if you examine yourself carefully, more often than not you will find that in reality you were afraid to say no because you *yourself* did not want to be hurt by the other person's reaction. You may have simply wanted him or her to like you. (You don't like everyone; why would you expect everyone to like you?) Or perhaps you said no initially, were pressured to say yes, and finally did. Such pressure is called control. Saying no once should be enough. When it's not, here's a handy response: "'No' is a complete sentence." This is also a handy response to the old emotionally dependent part of yourself, which may at times still tug at you to say yes when you mean no.

One way of saying yes when you mean no is to compromise. Compromise often means accepting lower standards than you would like. I suppose most people see such compromise as a necessary evil, or even as one of the hallmarks of a reasonable adult. I do not have much use for it, however. Too often, it is self-destructive. We compromise because we expect something back from the other person—probably something we should be providing for ourselves. If we are operating from a place of autonomy, expectations don't enter into it.

When I think of compromise, my mind goes first to personal relationships. In my own experience, I was always the one who compromised the most. What I gave up were pieces of my precious self, my integrity. I compromised because I thought that if I didn't, I would be alone. I didn't want to lose what I thought I had or wanted at the time. Eventually I lost it anyway, along with my self-worth. I finally learned that if someone said to me, "You're too good for me," I should believe it and walk away instead of trying to do my best to be less good—and too often achieving just that.

The more independent you become, the less inclined you will be to put up with nonsense in your personal or professional relationships, to put up with any person or situation that is not loving, respectful, and nurturing. Through your twelve-step practice, you learn to love yourself, and you know that your happiness rests between your two ears—not with another person.

Who Are You Now?

As you achieve independence, you will truly feel like a different person. Who are you now?

The power of self-identification is among the most important concepts I've encountered over the course of my own ongoing spiritual journey. The life you experience is a projection of your consciousness: you see what you believe. And whatever you attach to "I am" becomes a self-fulfilling belief.

So what are the consequences of saying, "I am a *recovering addict*"?

When you first say, "My name is . . . , and I am an addict," it is an important step. It is only when you stop the denial and face reality that change is possible. However, when you define yourself as "an addict" or, later, as "a recovering addict," you also define and even experience yourself as a disease. To eliminate the disease would be to eliminate yourself—not a very appealing outcome. The erroneous assumption, of course, is that the disease of addiction can't be healed, only treated, the best outcome being a perpetual state of recovery.

When you instead define yourself as "a person with an addiction," you define and experience yourself as an individual suffering from a condition, a state, not something integral to who you are. A condition can be healed. This shift in self-identification is an important next step.

And beyond that? Early on in my journey I also encountered the concept that, spiritually speaking, we are perfect. It had never occurred to me that I could be perfect on any level. I always thought I had to stop doing this, or start doing that, or be like so-and-so. But none of us needs to change, per se; we are born perfect. It is the conditioning that is imposed on us that is imperfect. As one teacher of Hinduism put it, "Perfection means . . . to be oneself—one's true self."[33] As you get better acquainted with your true self during the course of your spiritual journey, I expect that, like me, you will naturally cease to identify yourself as "a recovering fill-in-the-blank" and even as a person with an addiction.

• • • • •

As for me . . .

My name is Rosemary, and I am perfectly myself. Like you and almost everyone else, I was trained into addiction. Through continual practice of the twelve-step process described in this book, I unlearned

---

[33] Graham Ledgerwood, "Hinduism" (interview with Professor Satya Pal Sharma at East-West Cultural Center, Los Angeles; p. 15): accessed 18 Jul. 2014, http://www. spiritualworld.org/hinduism/spirit_perfect.htm.

the addictive behaviors that nearly destroyed me. In time, my reality became one not of recovery, but of discovery: I discovered, one day at a time, a true self I could love and a life I hadn't even known was possible. For many years now, I have been living that impossible, beautiful life. I have let nothing, no one, come between me and this healed life. And I never will.

Key Concepts

Independence The opposite of emotional dependency. Only when we become emotionally independent—able to meet our own emotional needs—can we be free of the need to control and manipulate others to get our needs met. Without independence, therefore, there is no love.

Inter-independence Inter-*in*dependence characterizes healthy relationships between people who are no longer driven by emotional dependency. It is only through independence that you can enjoy truly healthy relationships based on mutual regard.

Perfection A state of being your true self.

"Still by the Millions Dwelling"

O n the occasion of the forty-first anniversary of my sobriety, my son
Karl gave me *The Book That Started It All: The Original Working
Manuscript of Alcoholics Anonymous*. The volume includes a number of
primary documents, comments, write-ins, and so forth. Among these
is a speech Bill W. gave at the Texas State AA Convention on June 12,
1954. In it, he relates how, in 1937, he and "Smithy" were counting up
how many people had "stayed dry" with the help of their new program.
They realized that it was a handful—but a significant handful: "Bob
and I saw for the first time that this thing was going to succeed. That
God in his providence and mercy had thrown a new light into the dark
caves where we and our kind had been and were still by the millions
dwelling."[34]

I was struck by that last line's "dark caves." I don't know whether
Bill W. read Plato and meant to reference him, but my thoughts immediately went to the Greek philosopher's "Allegory of the Cave."[35]

It's written as a dialogue between Socrates (Plato's mentor) and
Glaucon, Plato's brother. Plato has Socrates describe a group of poor
souls who have lived in a cave all their lives, chained, with legs and
heads fixed, so as to face a blank wall. All they see of the world are shadows projected onto the wall by things passing in front of a fire behind
them. All they hear of it are echoes. They take the shadows and the
echoes to be the things themselves.

Plato argues through Socrates that if a prisoner were freed from
the cave, he would see—after a period of sunstruck confusion—that

---

[34] Anonymous, *The Book That Started It All: The Original Working Manuscript of
Alcoholics Anonymous* (Center City, MN: Hazelden Publishing, 2010), 205.

[35] *The Republic*, Book VII, 514a–520a.

what he thought was reality was a mere reflection of it. That the reality was not the darkness, but the light. Yet if this prisoner were to return to the cave, his attempts to enlighten his friends (to "carry this message to others," as Step Twelve would have it) might be unwelcome. The truth would upend everything they knew to be real, after all. They might even think him insane.

I like to think that I'm no more insane than Bill W. And that, standing on the shoulders of Bill and Bob and the other creators of the original Twelve Steps, I have brought to the caves a brighter light by which *all* those who suffer can guide themselves out. For the millions who still dwell deep in the caves of addiction, it is hard to believe another world exists. For the millions more who do not even recognize the addictive behaviors that chain them, the shadow world might not seem that bad. But the real world is *out here*. And a real life, lived in the light.

Glossary

This glossary explains, in abbreviated form, the key concepts discussed in this book. It's important to understand them *as defined here*—not as they may be traditionally defined. You may find it useful to turn here if you need reminding as you read or work the steps.

Abstinence Not synonymous with *healing*. Abstinence is more accurately described as behavior modification. It often coexists with *symptom substitution*. Knowing the difference between abstinence and healing can be a matter of life and death. If you have not recovered from the underlying *emotional dependency* that drives all *addictions,* you are not healed, and you are vulnerable to substituting an equally or more life-threatening addiction for your drug of choice.

Addict A person suffering from *addiction* has lost choice. He or she wants to permanently stop doing something self- or other-destructive, but can't. I avoid the word *addict*, by which we define and even experience ourselves as a disease. It also assumes a chronic condition that can't be healed, only treated, the best outcome being a perpetual state of *recovery*.

Addiction Any person, process, substance, or situation over which we have lost choice or believe we cannot live without. An addiction is one expression of *addictive behavior*. Anything that you use to alter your mood or avoid your feelings can become addictive. *Control* is the original addiction.

Addictive behavior Characterized by the complex of *fear, control, and manipulation.* Any attempt to use or control and manipulate that which is outside yourself—a person, process, substance, or situation—to meet internal needs. All addictive behaviors are symptoms of *emotional dependency.*

Algorithm Narrowly defined, an algorithm is a step-by-step procedure for solving a mathematical problem. More broadly, it's a step-by-step procedure for solving any problem or achieving some end. It outlines how, when, and in what order the steps must be done to achieve the desired result. A recipe is an algorithm. The Twelve Steps are an algorithm.

Catharsis The elimination of a complex—here, the complex of *fear, control, and manipulation*—by bringing it to consciousness and giving it expression. A result of the Fourth Step Algorithm and Step Five.

Control The imagined ability or power to manage, influence, or direct other people's behavior or the course of events. Control is an illusion, one as deeply unquestioned as it is consequential. It is the original *addiction*, from which all others flow. As Melody Beattie reminds us in *The Language of Letting Go*,[36] "Whatever we try to control does have control over us and our life." Thus my critical revision of Step One, from "admitted we were powerless over alcohol" (fill in your addiction) to "admitted we were powerless over life."

Dependency transformation The shift from dependency on a traditional God, on your own power, or on other people, places, situations, and things—none of which provided what you needed—to dependency on a power greater than yourself, within yourself. The outcome of this transformation is self-sufficiency and its accompanying empowerment, as opposed to other-dependency and its accompanying *powerlessness*.

Emotional dependency Reliance on that which is outside ourselves for our emotional needs. It occurs because as children we do not learn to meet our own needs; rather, we learn to be dependent on "the other" (person, substance, situation) to meet them. It's a using mentality. Triggers *addictive behavior*, i.e., *fear, control, and manipulation*.

Expectation Expectations can be symptomatic of unhealthy *emotional dependency*. They tend to generate *fear, control, and manipulation*. You are powerless over anyone or anything but yourself, so to have expectations of other people, things, or situations is to invite *resentment*. No expectations = no disappointment = no resentment.

Faith Even if you are an atheist, you have faith of one kind or another. You have faith in whatever you give your power to: people, things, ideas,

---

[36] Melody Beattie, *The Language of Letting Go* (Center City, MN: Hazelden, 1990).

situations, prejudices. Many of us give our power to fear, which is simply faith in negativity. Optimism is faith in positivity. Take your pick, but I suggest the latter. Experience is, not always but often, faith realized.

Fear, control, and manipulation A survival mechanism; also known as *addictive behavior*. When we fear that we will not get what we need or want, this fear triggers control and manipulation of "the other" (person, substance, or situation) in an attempt to get it. When the object of our *emotional dependency* is withdrawn (or threatened to be), fear, control, and manipulation become even more intense, in proportion to the intensity of the dependency—our control efforts spin out of control. A recipe for *insanity*. Self-control is the only control that works.

God Also known as your higher power or higher self. If God is infinite—as almost any notion of God would have it—then nothing is outside of God. We are all parts of the whole. There is no "other"; "God" is you. I came to think of God as simply the good in me: the old Saxon word for *good* is spelled *g-o-d,* and Plato, in his "Allegory of the Cave," describes "the Good" as "the cause of all that is correct and beautiful in anything."

Healing It's much more than *abstinence,* although abstinence is required for healing. Within the context of *addictive behavior,* healing is a process that produces a qualitative change in the consciousness of the addicted person. This change restores choice. That is, it restores the ability to choose to avoid or disengage from any addictive behavior as it surfaces. The destination of healing is wholeness—a self-reliant state of being in which we can fully express ourselves spiritually, emotionally, intellectually, physically, and creatively, and therefore productively and financially. It's a return to the self-actualization we knew at the very beginning of our lives.

Honesty An antidote to *addictive behavior.* Lying is an addictive behavior—a manifestation of the complex of *fear, control, and manipulation.* We are trained to lie, and we carry the model into adulthood. All addictive behavior promotes further addictive behavior, so the eventual outcome of lying is the practice of multiple addictions. Honesty is a measure of *healing* in that we are honest in direct ratio to our self-reliance.

Independence Also known as healthy self-reliance. The opposite of *emotional dependency.* Independence is one result of *healing.* If you want to know whether you are independent, see how often you say yes when you want to say no, or no when you want to say yes. Only when we become emotionally independent—able to meet our own emotional needs—can we be free of the need to control and manipulate others to get our needs met. Without independence, therefore, there is no *love*.

Insanity Within the context of *addictive behavior*, insanity can be defined as the belief that you have any control over that which is outside yourself. It's the continual attempt to get your needs met through control and manipulation of externals. See also *sanity*.

Inter-independence Inter-*de*pendence characterizes unhealthy relationships; the parties are driven by *emotional dependency* as individuals and are engaged in *addictive behavior*. Inter-*in*dependence characterizes healthy relationships between people who are no longer driven by emotional dependency. It is only through *independence* that you can enjoy truly healthy relationships based on mutual regard.

Love Love is love. It has no opposite. If it's "conditional," it's not love; it's control and manipulation (see *fear, control, and manipulation*). For instance, what is called a love-hate relationship has nothing to do with love. It is more accurately described as a control/manipulation–hate relationship. When one person's *expectations* are not met, control and manipulation kick in. When those efforts do not have the desired results, hate comes into play.

Moral In this context, what's moral is whatever is good for your morale, or sense of well-being. Many of the moral principles that form your conscience are not eternal truths but rather received "wisdom"—more externals that you've become dependent on. They may in fact not be moral. That is, they may not be good for you or those around you.

Parenting As practiced across most families, cultures, and times, parenting teaches *emotional dependency* and is therefore the root cause of *addictive behavior*. It is designed to meet the needs of parents, who were themselves raised to be emotionally dependent, and is therefore characterized not by *love* but by *fear, control, and manipulation*. Given the imperative of control—the original addiction—parenting's primary goal is obedience, which is realized through rewards and punishments.

Perfection Spiritually speaking, we are born perfect; none of us needs to change, per se. It is the conditioning that is imposed on us that is imperfect. As one teacher of Hinduism put it, "Perfection means . . . to be oneself—one's true self."

Powerlessness Ultimately, we are powerless over that which is outside ourselves. For this reason, the strategy of control and manipulation (see *fear, control, and manipulation*) is pointless, a recipe for *insanity*. Recognizing this powerlessness (Step One, as modified in this book) is the beginning of self-empowerment.

Psychology Traditionally defined as a science that deals with the mind and with mental and emotional processes, and disorders and dysfunctions thereof. Not mentioned in any standard definition, or in most discussion of psychotherapy, is that the root of the word, *psyche,* means "soul." I believe we must embrace this; what I propose in this book is a form of soul, or spiritual, therapy.

Recovery Mistakenly defined by most people as *abstinence,* or sobriety. The assumption is that without drugs, *sanity* returns. However, the drive to self-destruct simply shifts from chemicals to some other progressively *addictive behavior.* Thus "recovery" becomes a "re-covering," or covering over, of the dominant *addiction* with secondary addictions (see *symptom substitution*).

Relapse Slip, backslide, fall off the wagon. It's what happens when you can't stay stopped. The unfortunate norm in twelve-step programs. Traditionally defined as a return to using the substance of choice; in truth, the substitution of a second, third, or fourth choice (of any *addictive behavior*) in order to maintain *abstinence* from the first is a form of relapse. (See *symptom substitution.*) Relapse begins before the behavior itself does, with the very impulse to control and manipulate (see *fear, control, and manipulation*).

Religion "A personal set or institutionalized system of . . . attitudes, beliefs, and practices,"[37] or a commitment to such a system. Any given

---

[37] *Merriam-Webster's Collegiate Dictionary,* 11th Edition (Springfield, MA, 2004), 1051.

religious practice may or may not promote *spirituality*. But even if it does, it is not the thing itself.

Resentment A resentment is any emotional trauma, real or imaginary, that is not only "re-sent" in consciousness but also re-felt (the Old French *sentir* means to feel), through rumination or conversation. My dictionary defines resentment as "a feeling of indignant displeasure or persistent ill-will at something regarded as a wrong, insult, or injury."[38] I define it as an unfulfilled *expectation*. It occurs when your attempts to control and manipulate externals (people, substances, or situations) are frustrated. Dealing with resentments is a major thrust of the Fourth Step Algorithm.

Responsibility As in "response-ability": your willingness and *ability* to *respond* to life—to be responsible for yourself in all areas of your life—rather than depend on others to respond for you. Responsibility is what frees you from the ideas, desires, whims, and approval of others, so that you may pursue your own unadulterated version of fulfillment.

Sanity A learned state of mental soundness that includes the ability to anticipate and appraise the effects of your actions. Mental soundness is a prerequisite for bodily health. Many people have never known true sanity. This twelve-step process is one way to learn it. See also *insanity*.

Spirituality Sensitivity to the spiritual, or a state of being spiritual. That which is spiritual is that which is life giving: that which promotes wholeness, not holiness. Not the same thing as *religion*.

Symptom substitution The substitution of one form of *addictive behavior* for another (for example, sugar for alcohol or dieting for overeating). Addicted people who are practicing symptom substitution often appear to be practicing *abstinence*, but they are actually in *relapse*. All *addictions* are symptoms of a single underlying problem, *emotional dependency*; therefore they serve the same function and are in practice more or less interchangeable.

---

[38] Ibid., 1059.

The Brown Method, Outlined

This appendix outlines the step process as modified in this book, including the Fourth Step Algorithm. If you are a person who, like me, can become overwhelmed when faced with a quantity of text, you may find it helpful to refer to this once you have read the book and are actually working through the steps. The page numbers refer you to the full discussion of the step.

Step One *Page 42*

We admitted we were powerless over life—people, situations, circumstances, and substances—and that our lives and our minds were unmanageable when we tried to control any part of it.

Step Two *Page 43*

Came to believe that a power greater than ourselves could help us find sanity.

Step Three *Page 45*

Made a decision to turn our will and our lives, and the lives of others, over to the care of this power—the God of our understanding.

Step Four *Page 46*

Made a searching and fearless moral inventory of all relationships.

The Fourth Step Algorithm *Page 63*

Basic Rules:

- Work is to be done daily for twenty to thirty minutes.
- Work is to be handwritten, during daylight hours.

- You will contact your facilitator as often as seven days a week or as few as one—per his or her judgment—for five to fifteen minutes (by phone, email, or other convenient method).
- Barring illness or other unexpected events, if you choose not to do the work three days in a row, fail to contact your facilitator as agreed, or fail to pay as agreed, the therapy will end.

Phase 1: List your relationships, Page 73 Every person (yourself included) who has ever caused you to feel hurt in any way.

Phase 2: List incidents and feelings, Page 76 Any and all hurtful incidents that occurred in your relationships, and how you felt at the time.

Phase 3: List needs, wants, and expectations, Page 78 Look at all the incidents uncovered in phase two to explore why you felt hurt at the time—usually because of an unmet need, want, or expectation.

Phase 4: Review your sex life, Page 81 Make the same lists you did in phases one, two, and three, in order to uncover anything you missed with regard to sex. Then explore the following set of questions paraphrased from the *Twelve and Twelve* (pages 50–52), in writing:

1. Did my pursuit of sex hurt others? Who? How?
2. Did I hurt my marriage and/or my children?
3. Did I hurt myself?
4. Did I risk my standing with friends, neighbors, or colleagues?
5. Did I feel guilty?
6. Did I absolve myself by maintaining that I was not the pursuer?
7. How did I react to sexual frustration?
8. Did I take frustration out on others?
9. If things weren't good at home, did I use that to excuse promiscuity?
10. What sexual situations made me anxious, bitter, frustrated, or depressed?
11. Looking at each situation, can I see emotional dependency at play?
12. If these problems really were caused by the behavior of others, why did I accept the behavior?

Phase 5: Review your work and finances, Page 84 Explore the following set of questions paraphrased from the *Twelve and Twelve* (pages 51–52), in writing:

1. Have my addiction of choice and other addictive behaviors contributed to financial problems?
2. Have I let fear and doubt about my performance at work destroy my confidence?
3. If I ever felt inadequate, did I try to cover it up by lying or avoiding responsibility?
4. Or did I exaggerate my abilities, acting like a bigshot?
5. Have I had such unprincipled ambition that I undermined others?
6. Have I been extravagant with money?
7. Have I recklessly borrowed money, with no thought to repaying it?
8. Have I been cheap, failing to support my family as I should?
9. Have I cut corners financially?
10. What about "quick money," the stock market, or gambling?
11. To what extent has my emotional dependency created issues with work and money?
12. If these problems really have been caused by the behavior of others, why have I accepted the behavior?
13. If I can't change my work or financial circumstances at this time, am I willing to do something to shape my life to conditions as they are?

Phase 6: List principles, institutions, and fears, Page 85

Phase 7: List the good, Page 87 All that you like and love about yourself, all that other people have told you they like and love about you (whether or not you believe it), and all that you feel you've done right in your life.

Step Five *Page 52*

Admitted to God, to ourselves, and to another human being the exact nature of our relationships.

Step Six *Page 56*

Were entirely ready to leave our defective conditioning behind.

Step Seven *Page 56*

Humbly asked God to help us do this.

Step Eight *Page 57*

Made a list of all persons we had harmed, including ourselves, and became willing to make amends to them all.

Step Nine *Page 58*

Made direct amends to such people wherever possible, except when to do so would injure them or others.

Step Ten *Page 59*

Continued to take personal inventory and when we were wrong promptly admitted it.

Remember that your inventory includes any wrongs you have suffered—and recognition of the role you may have played, via any lingering emotional dependency, in creating the experience.

Step Eleven *Page 60*

Sought through prayer or meditation to improve our conscious contact with the God of our understanding, seeking only knowledge of God's will for us and the power to carry that out.

Step Twelve *Page 61*

Having had a spiritual awakening as the result of these steps, we tried to carry this message to others and to practice these principles in all areas of our lives.

Appendix B

Self-evaluation of Independence

Regular self-analysis is an important part of developing an independent life. The questions below may help you evaluate and further your progress.

I suggest that you first quickly read through them all to get more familiar with the full dimensions of independence; this may help you see which areas of your life need special attention. Then work through each relevant section over time, or as issues come up.

Self-evaluation of Personal Independence

Spiritual independence:

1. Do I allow an external authority to determine my religious beliefs?
2. Do I engage in a self-determined spiritual practice on most days?
3. Do I reject thoughts, words, actions, and reactions that are not life giving?
4. Are the people I regularly spend time with supportive and nurturing?
5. Do they make me laugh?
6. Do I question authority? If so, whose and in what ways?

Emotional independence:

1. Am I in touch with my own feelings and needs?
2. Am I taking personal responsibility for satisfying my needs?
3. In what ways, on a daily basis, do I love myself, give to myself, and show myself that I value and admire myself?
4. Do I refrain from comparing myself to others?
5. Do I still need approval from others?
6. Do I allow myself to be unnecessarily drawn into stressful conversations and situations?
7. Is my self-esteem based on who I am (as it should be), instead of what I do?
8. Am I overly dependent on others for emotional support?
9. For those times when I genuinely need the emotional support of others, do I have a circle of trusted people to turn to, or am I overly dependent on one or two people, or on my family?
10. Do I feel responsible to or for anyone else (besides children and the infirm)?
11. Do I fear abandonment?

Intellectual independence:

1. Do I think for myself, or do I allow others to think for me and make decisions for me?
2. How am I growing intellectually on a daily basis? What am I learning?
3. What are my immediate goals?
4. Is my work creative and satisfying?
5. If I am unhappy with my job, what are my immediate plans for either improving the situation or moving on to something better?
6. Is my standard for excellence internal rather than external?
7. Is my self-worth independent of both praise and criticism?

Physical independence:

1. Am I in touch with my physical needs, and do I honor them?
2. Do I make my physical well-being a priority each day?

3. Do I schedule enough time for exercise each day/week?
4. Do I get enough sleep?
5. Do I make time for healthful meals?
6. Do I eat the kinds and amounts of foods that make me feel my best, or do I follow someone else's regimen or idea of what's best for my body?

Economic independence:

1. Am I supporting myself financially? Who pays my bills?
2. Do I have a budget?
3. What are my financial goals?
4. How much money do I save?
5. Do I put aside money for fun, for vacation?
6. How much do I give to charity?
7. Do I still have fears about my financial security?
8. If I need to learn more about money, am I reading about it, seeking expert advice, and putting into practice what I am learning?

If I am in a partner relationship . . .

1. Who controls the money?
2. Do I have my own money?
3. Does my partner have his/her own money?
4. If I do not have an income-producing job, how do I detemine what money is my own?
5. If I want to buy something, do I feel I have to ask permission, or do we have a comfortable agreement about purchases?
6. Do I feel guilty about spending money that I did not earn outside the home?
7. If we both work outside the home, are we sharing the household expenses in an equitable way?

Self-evaluation of Abuse

Independence is characterized by neither taking nor giving abuse of any kind, directly or indirectly. We accept abuse for fear that if we don't, we'll lose or not get what we think we need or want; we abuse to get our own way or to stop others from doing what they want to do. Many instances of abuse can be dealt with simply by walking away.

Am I engaged in or subject to . . .

Spiritual abuse Any kind of put-down, including destructive criticism and judgments of self and others. Think about what it means to "put down" an animal. A put-down is a killing blow to the spirit. Perfectionism is a kind of continuous, self-inflicted put-down.

Emotional abuse Any violation of emotional boundaries. Whenever your unique emotional reality is discounted or denied, you are being abused. With regard to children, they have a need for and a right to love, affection, attention, direction, and support and in fact must have these to complete their emotional development; withholding of this love constitutes abuse.

- Violent language
- Sarcasm
- Destructive criticism
- Threats of rejection
- Pressure to say yes when the answer was no
- Withdrawal of affection and/or attention
- The silent treatment
- Neglect
- Threats of abandonment ("If you do/don't do that, I'll leave")

Intellectual abuse Intellectual abuse occurs when someone's opinions or ideas are ignored, discounted, or ridiculed. We all have an innate right to think for ourselves, formulate our own opinions, puzzle things out, and make mistakes; when those intellectual processes are interrupted or interfered with, that is abuse.

Physical abuse Anything done to someone's body without his or her consent. Period. A fist in the face is obviously abusive, but physical abuse can be quite casual and insidious. Tickling, for example, can be torturous, rendering someone helpless. Compelling a child to kiss or hug a relative that he or she does not want to be affectionate with is another example of subtle, socially acceptable abuse.

Sexual abuse Any sexual invasion of either physical or emotional boundaries, ranging from the overt (rape) to the covert (sexual innuendo, deprivation of privacy).

Economic abuse Any withdrawal or threatened withdrawal of financial support unless the one supported agrees to conditions.

Self-evaluation of Honesty

1. When was the last time I lied? Told a partial truth? Exaggerated or embellished the truth?
2. If I did lie, did I make amends immediately or as soon as I realized it?
3. Do I usually say yes when I want to say yes, and no when I want to say no? Or do I continue to do what others want—to make them happy, to keep the peace, or to get what I want from them?
4. Do I experience yes and no as responses of equal value, "no" being free of emotional baggage?
5. If I am asked a direct question, do I give a direct answer?
6. Do I continue to associate with people I don't like, or people whose company I simply don't enjoy? If so, why?
7. Do I gossip? Why?

Self-evaluation of Identity

1. Whatever I attach to "I am" is my identity. How do I finish "I am . . ." ?
2. What images and thoughts about myself am I feeding energy into? Is that the identity I want to grow?
3. Do I trust myself?
4. What are my spiritual beliefs?
5. What are my core values?
6. When I look at my checkbook or credit card statement, does my spending (which reflects my actual priorities) reflect my values?

Self-evaluation of Relationships

Are you moving away from inter-*de*pendence to inter-*in*dependence in your relationships?

1. Are my relationships prioritized, with spiritual relationships at the foundation?

Relationships with others

Relationship to work—
a creative, productive endeavor

Relationship with oneself

Spiritual relationships—relationships to
whatever is perceived as life giving

2. Do I care for myself first, recognizing that only then will my responsibility toward others be clear and expressed in healthy ways?
3. Am I minimally concerned with how others behave, dress, eat, and spend money?
4. Do I mind my own business, allowing others to solve their own problems?
5. Do I help others only when asked? (Helping is the sunny side of control.)
6. Do I try to tell others what they should or should not do?
7. Do I give unsolicited advice?
8. Am I involved in others' crises and melodrama?
9. Do I give only what I have to give?
10. Do I give without conditions or expectations, without using the giving to control anyone?
11. Does spending time alone feel like precious solitude instead of isolation or loneliness?
12. Do I express anger in appropriate ways?
13. Do I accept anger in myself and others as being human and just as valuable as other feelings?

14. Do I have a low tolerance for inappropriate behavior in myself and others?

Self-evaluation of Balance

A balanced life is one sign of healthy self-governance. Balance, however, looks different for everyone. You must figure out for yourself what it means for you—which is a much easier task when, as a result of my step method, you know who you are and what you need to be happy and healthy.

One way to self-evaluate in this area is to keep precise track of how you spend your time every day for a week. Keep a little notebook with you (or, if you're so inclined, you can try keeping track with a phone app). At the end of the week, put everything in categories and add up the totals. Just like your checkbook, this "balance sheet" will tell you whether your actions match your values. You might be surprised. Here are some categories you might include:

Sleep	Dishes	Email	TV
Bathing	Family	Internet	News
Work	Laundry	Socializing	Reading
Commute	Cleaning	Exercise	Writing
Other driving	Groceries	Meditation	Hobby
Eating	Shopping	Prayer	Finances
Food prep	Phone/texting	Movies	Volunteering

Algorithms for Problem Solving

An algorithm is a step-by-step procedure for solving a problem or achieving an end. Here are two simple ones, not for specific problems, but for approaching problems in general. Work with them in writing.

General Problems

1. What is the problem?
2. Define the problem in detail.
3. List and consider all the factors that contribute to it.
4. List the steps you can take to solve it.
5. Which of those steps are you willing to take?
6. If you are unwilling to act on the options at this time, accept your unwillingness, stop talking about the problem, and turn your attention to constructively living your life.

Relationship Problems

The approach is similar to that for general problems but incorporates aspects of the Fourth Step Algorithm:

1. What is the situation?
2. Define the situation in detail: Who was involved? What was said or done, or not said or done?
3. What did/do you think and feel?
4. Why were/are you upset?
5. Were you afraid you would lose what you thought you had or not get what you thought you wanted?
6. Was it because of an unfulfilled expectation?
7. Were you disappointed in yourself or the other person?

8. Did reality fail to measure up to your picture of how it "should" be?
9. Were you depending on something or someone outside yourself to make you happy?

If the answer to one or more of questions 5 through 9 is yes, then, in recognizing your co-creation of the problem, you have solved it.

Remember the first of the modified Twelve Steps: "We admitted we were powerless over life—people, situations, circumstances, substances—and that our lives and our minds were unmanageable when we tried to control any part of it."

Big Book and
Twelve and Twelve References

If you want to see the origins of the Fourth Step Algorithm, the pertinent section of *Alcoholics Anonymous,* aka the Big Book, is chapter 5, "How It Works," and of *Twelve Steps and Twelve Traditions,* "Step Four." Below are the references to the primary passages I drew from (Big Book page numbers refer to the fourth edition), some followed by a key phrase or two.

Alcoholics Anonymous, fourth edition, and *Twelve Steps and Twelve Traditions* are both published by Alcoholics Anonymous World Services Inc. (New York, 2002).

Phase 1: List your Relationships

· The Big Book, pages 64–65: "In dealing with resentments, we set them on paper. We listed people, institutions or principles with whom we were angry."

Phase 6: List Institutions, Principles, and Fears

· The Big Book, pages 64–65: "In dealing with resentments, we set them on paper. We listed people, institutions or principles with whom we were angry."
· The Big Book, pages 67–68: "We reviewed our fears thoroughly. We put them on paper, even though we had no resentment in connection with them."

Phase 3: List Your Needs, Wants, and Expectations

· The Big Book, pages 65–67: "We turned back to the list, for it held the key to the future. We were prepared to look at it from an entirely different angle. . . . we resolutely looked for our own mistakes."

Phase 4: Review Your Sex Life

- The Big Book, pages 68–70: "We subjected each relation to this test—was it selfish or not?"
- The *Twelve and Twelve,* pages 50–52

Phase 5: Review Your Work and Finances

- The *Twelve and Twelve,* pages 51–52

Step Five

- The Big Book, page 68: "Self-reliance was good as far as it went, but it didn't go far enough."
- The Big Book, pages 72–73: "We usually find a solitary self-appraisal insufficient."

Index

About the Author

Dr. Rosemary Ellsworth Brown is a psychologist. She graduated from Smith College as an Ada Comstock Scholar in 1989 and completed her doctorate in counseling psychology at the Union Institute in 1993. Her academic research focused on relapse, in particular on why AA and its myriad Twelve Step offshoots proved ineffective for the majority of their members.

Dr. Brown's research has been not only academic and professional in nature, but also personal. She attended her first AA meeting in 1968, stayed sober for a year, and then experienced a tragic two-year relapse. She returned to the program determined to understand and solve the problem of relapse and devoted the rest of her professional life, and much of her personal life, to doing so.

Ultimately, she identified the primary cause of all addictive behaviors and modified the Twelve Steps to address it, eliminating their traditional symptom focus and trial-and-error aspect. She has been using her step method to heal the cause of addictive behavior and prevent relapse among her clients and sponsees for upwards of thirty years.

Dr. Brown is now at work on her autobiography.